THE QEMANT
A pagan-Hebraic peasantry of Ethiopia

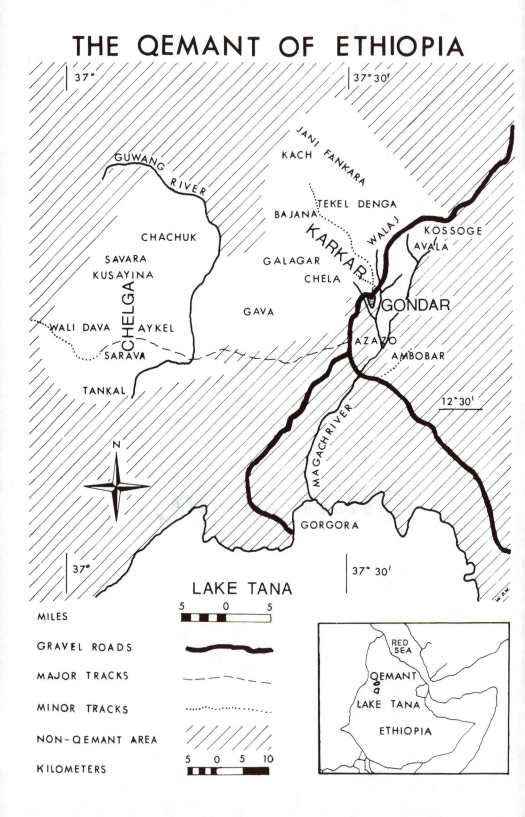

THE QEMANT OF ETHIOPIA

37°
37° 30'

GUWANG RIVER

JANI FANKARA
KACH

TEKEL DENGA
BAJANA
KARKAR
CHACHUK
WALAJ
KOSSOGE
SAVARA
GALAGAR
AVALÁ
KUSAYINA
CHELA
CHELGA
GAVA
GONDAR
WALI DAVA
AYKEL
AZAZO
SARAVA
AMBOBAR

TANKAL

12° 30'

N

MAGACH RIVER

GORGORA

37°
37° 30'

LAKE TANA

MILES

5   0   5

GRAVEL ROADS

MAJOR TRACKS

MINOR TRACKS

NON-QEMANT AREA

KILOMETERS

5   0   5   10

RED
SEA

QEMANT

LAKE TANA

ETHIOPIA

W.O.W.

THE QEMANT

A Pagan-Hebraic Peasantry of Ethiopia

By

FREDERICK C. GAMST
University of Massachusetts, Boston

WAVELAND
PRESS, INC.
Prospect Heights, Illinois

For information about this book, write or call:

Waveland Press, Inc.
P.O. Box 400
Prospect Heights, Illinois 60070
(847) 634-0081

Cover photograph: *Higher priest (left) and lower priest (right) preparing sacred beer and blessed seeds for rite of spring.*

To Marilou

Foreword

About the Author

Frederick C. Gamst is professor of anthropology at the University of Massachusetts, Boston. He received his B.A. "with highest honors" from the University of California at Los Angeles and his Ph.D. from the University of California at Berkeley. In addition to fieldwork in Ethiopia, he has made extensive studies of railroaders in the United States.

About the Book

This is a study of an ancient culture in Ethiopia, a land relatively little known to Western students. The Qemant speak a dialect of the Cushitic language, are Caucasoid, and practice a religion composed of syncretized pagan and Hebraic elements, with a few Christian features. The Hebraism is an ancient form, unaffected by Hebraic religious change of the last two millennia. The Agaw, of whom the Qemant are a division, were the original inhabitants of northern and central Ethiopia. Since Qemant culture was influenced by ancient Christianity prior to the coming of Islam, it has, with its ancient Hebraic characteristics, a special significance in the perspective of Western culture history. The Qemant are also of special significance to anthropologists as an example of a peasantry unaffected by modernization, and as an example of acculturation brought about by other than Euro-American culture. The Qemant are being Amharized, not Westernized, as the dominant and surrounding Amhara society of Ethiopia exerts a determinant influence. Amharization began in the thirteenth century, but due to the strong cultural boundary maintenance, in substantial part the result of the definition of the culture given by the religious system, the Qemant have, until now, been able to resist assimilation.

Dr. Gamst has written a scholarly book that will be useful to students of Western culture history as well as to anthropologists interested in a wider variety of the world's cultures. He has also written an interesting book enlivened by attention to individuals and specific events that illustrate impersonal generalizations. He occasionally allows his own experience and reactions to appear, giving the reader a sharpened sense of reality as Qemant culture is described.

GEORGE AND LOUISE SPINDLER

Preface

Beginning in September 1964, I conducted fourteen months of ethnographic fieldwork in Ethiopia. Twelve months were spent among the Qemant, a previously unstudied division of the Agaw peoples, in the Governor Generalate, or province, of Bagemder and Semen. This book is based upon the fieldwork and has been written as a brief introduction to the Qemant and to their religion, which I view as the focal point of the Qemant way of life and of the factors that have inhibited cultural change among this people.

My study was conducted principally in a community called Karkar, until recently the chief religious center of the Qemant. A briefer study was made at the community of Chelga, a religious center once slightly less important than Karkar, but now the only religious center of the Qemant. I also visited most of the forty or more other Qemant communities at one time or another. Ethnographic surveys were made of other groups of the Agaw, including the Falasha, who are scattered throughout the province of Bagemder and Semen, the Awiya, in Gojjam province south of Bagemder and Semen, and the Wayto of Lake Tana.

I am deeply indebted to the Foreign Area Fellowship Program of the Joint Committee of the Social Science Research Council and the American Council of Learned Societies for financial support of the fieldwork. Acknowledgment is also due to Rice University for a grant-in-aid of research during the summer of 1967 and to the Center for Research on Social Change and Economic Development of Rice University for a grant-in-aid of research during the summer of 1968. These grants enabled me to investigate further published materials on Ethiopia and to prepare the manuscript for this book.

The study was completed with the cooperation and aid of the Imperial Ethiopian Government, to which I am grateful. It is impossible to list all of the many government officials on national, provincial, and local levels who gave their full cooperation and hospitality. I would like to thank specially the Ethiopian Studies Institute of the Haile Selassie I University, located in Addis Ababa and directed by Dr. Richard Pankhurst, for the courtesies shown and aid rendered to me. Mr. Stanislaw Chojnacki of the Institute was particularly friendly and helpful, as was Dr. Dennis Carlson of the Haile Selassie I Public Health College, located in Gondar. Gratitude is due also to the many Ethiopians in the countryside who received me graciously and gave help of many kinds that allowed my fieldwork to progress smoothly.

Special thanks go to my wife Marilou for her constant encouragement and assistance in the field and in the writing of this book, and to my assistant in the field, Alamayehu Gesese, for his invaluable aid. I also wish to acknowledge the guidance and support of Edward Norbeck in all stages of the preparation of this book, and the help of George M. Foster and William Bascom with earlier drafts of this study.

Houston, Texas
August 1969

FREDERICK C. GAMST

Contents

THE QEMANT

A Pagan-Hebraic Peasantry of Ethiopia

Introduction

T HE QEMANT, an ethnic group with an estimated population of 20,000 to 25,000, are a remnant of the Cushitic-speaking Agaw peoples, the original inhabitants of northern and central Ethiopia. Their enclave, which we shall call Qemantland, lies within a fairly rugged region of the temperate and verdant high plateau of Ethiopia and is located north of Lake Tana, the source of the Blue Nile, and surrounding the town of Gondar, the national capital of several centuries ago. (The /q/ in the word *Qemant* and in other Ethiopian words represents a glottalized or "explosive" /k/ sound, but the reader may simply pronounce it as he would the English /k/.)

Qemantland does not have compact villages. Instead, one to four wattle-and-daub walled houses topped by peaked thatch roofs constitute semi-isolated homesteads that are scattered across pastures and cultivated fields throughout the length and breadth of the land. Anywhere from one to four hundred of these homesteads are united socially to form a widely dispersed community.

The Land

The appearance of Qemantland changes with the seasons. Under the leaden skies of the summer rainy season, the landscape is dull; the ground is a swampy morass and streams are swollen, dangerous, chocolate-brown torrents. During the close of and immediately following the rainy season, cultivated fields abound with sprouting crops in several hues of green. Pale blue flowers of the flax plant and golden-yellow flowers of another cultivated oil seed stud the landscape. Bright yellow wildflowers dot the pastures and the steep hillslopes, which in this season are covered with lush grass. Streams are full and crystal clear.

As the dry season approaches, the soil firms, streams subside, and crops begin to ripen, turning the landscape into a mosaic of amber and gold. Flat-topped acacia trees, their crowns laden with either pink or off-white blossoms, stand starkly against the azure skies. Late in the dry season cultivated fields lie barren, hard, and brown; pastures are yellowed and dried. All but the largest streams are reduced to series of stagnant green pools awaiting the return of the rains so they can continue their flow to Lake Tana. The waters of Tana, muddy with the soils of Qemantland and other Ethiopian areas, eventually overflow into the great, silt-laden Blue Nile and help cut a mile-deep canyon across Ethiopia before they join the White Nile for a journey across arid Sudan and Egypt to the Mediterranean Sea.

The fertile soils of Qemantland support an economy based upon agricultural technology, including the plow, draft animals, and other livestock which are secondary to the crops in the subsistence pattern. Cereals, legumes, oil seeds, and root crops are the staples of the economy, some being first domesticated as early as five thousand years ago by the ancestors of the Qemant.

Are the Qemant Peasants?

The Qemant are called peasants in this work because they are cultivators who produce a small surplus partially exchanged in marketplaces and partially paid as taxes to maintain members of a literate secular and clerical administrative hierarchy of the Ethiopian civilization. Ethiopia's civilization is a southern extension of the preindustrial civilization of the Mediterranean and Near Eastern region which began to emerge about six thousand years ago in western Asia as an outgrowth of the Agricultural Revolution, but did not diffuse to Ethiopia until a little under three thousand years ago.

In this and other respects the Qemant represent a civilization like the one that preceded our modern industrial-urban society. By studying the Qemant we not only learn some of the cultural variation found in little-known Ethiopia but we also become familiar with the only region in which the Christian civilization present in the Middle East and North Africa before the coming of Islam still survives. Most important, by investigating the Qemant we acquire knowledge of one of the few peasantries in the world as yet almost completely unaffected and out of touch with the globe-encircling forces of modernization, including industrialization. The Qemant are today undergoing marked cultural change, not toward the Western model of culture, but toward the patterns of culture of the Amhara peasantry surrounding them.

Preindustrial civilization is more socially complex and technologically advanced than primitive societies of hunters and gatherers and horticulturalists. It is characterized by urbanism, writing, plow agriculture, metallurgy, monumental buildings and at least two basic societal components. By this last term we mean a society consisting in part of an elite, often in an urban setting, with an elaborate high culture, or Great Tradition, based upon literacy. The other component consists of a large rural population of peasants, that is, cultivators and some artisans, with a Little Tradition, or a folk manifestation of the Great Tradition modified by passage of time and usually by reinterpretation in the rustic setting. A civilization is organized politically into a state, or states, and the power-wielding elite in control also govern and guide the lives of the peasants. In turn, the peasants provide most of the wealth and labor necessary for the perpetuation and maintenance of the state and the elite.

The Qemant peasants have been politically subordinate, for at least the last six hundred years, to the elite of the much larger Amhara and Tegre ethnic groups of Ethiopia, each with its own peasantry. Nevertheless, the Qemant have been allowed a large measure of internal political autonomy. For this reason their indigenous hierarchy of politicoreligious leaders persisted in almost unmodified form until the end of the nineteenth century, and it continues in attenuated form to this day. The indigenous political structure of the Qemant, which serves as an integrative factor among them, has three levels: councils of elders on the lowest level, higher and lower priests in intermediate positions, and the *wambar,* the arch politicoreligious leader, at the apex. The wambar acknowledges the secular sovereignty of the Amhara administrators who have social positions and roles within an ascending hierarchy of authority constituting what might be termed a feudal system. The use of the term "feudal" in this book closely parallels the use of the word by historians, who employ it to mean relationships of lord and vassal such as once existed in Europe. Indeed the feudal system of Christian Ethiopia, which persists largely unmodified to this day, is similar to the feudal system once prevalent in Christian Europe.

Integrative Factors

The indigenous political system of the Qemant is not the only integrative factor among them. They are also united by bonds of kinship extending beyond the confines of individual homesteads and linking together their widely dispersed communities. The males of each homestead are closely related through paternal lines to one another and to males in some of the nearby homesteads in their community. The paternal lines lead back to the oldest living male among them or to an ancestor of these men from one or two generations earlier. These paternal lines can be traced back through time, along with many other such lines of descent from part of the remainder of the community and from parts of other Qemant communities, until they ultimately merge into the person of a culture hero who is the common ancestor of this vast number of men and the founder of the clan to which they belong. Therefore, a clan is a kinship group whose members trace descent unilineally, through the line of one parent—in this case, the male line—to an ancestor who is usually mythical.

The many Qemant clans, each composed of several lineages, or segments of the clan, are united on a greater structural level to form two moieties, a fundamental dual social division into which an ethnic group may be organized. All Qemant belong to either one or the other of the two moieties, and they must marry, according to Qemant marriage laws, outside of their own moiety and into the other one; these moieties are therefore exogamous.

The unique and interesting Qemant religion is a syncretized and archaic form of belief. Three religious strata exist in the northern and central parts of

A Qemant family spanning sixty-five years and three generations. The iron-sinewed plowman at the right continues to cultivate his field despite his age. His wife may walk twenty kilometers each way to and from a market place in a single day. Note wattle-and-daub walled house.

highland Ethiopia. (The relatively recent intrusion of Islam to some of the people of these parts of Ethiopia need not be considered here.) The oldest stratum consists of several varieties of the religious beliefs of the ancestors of the present-day Agaw peoples of Ethiopia and may be called pagan-Agaw. A more recent stratum is the Hebrew religion, which diffused to northern Ethiopia about twenty centuries ago or more, and still more recent is the sixteen-century-old Monophysite Christianity now adhered to by about one-quarter to one-third of all Ethiopians.

The religion of the Qemant is largely pagan-Agaw, but many Hebraic elements and a bare trace of Christian characteristics are also found, making the Qemant religion pagan-Hebraic. The Hebraism found among the Qemant is an ancient form, unaffected by Hebraic religious change of the past two millennia. This Hebraism is dominant in the religion of the Falasha, neighbors of the Qemant who are also an Agaw people and sometimes called "the Black Jews of Ethiopia." The religion of the Falasha also retains pronounced manifestations of the pagan-Agaw substratum and is Hebrao-pagan rather than solely Hebraic. I realize the essence of Hebraism is monotheism, but even beliefs centering upon Hebraic monotheism can become syncretized with other patterns of religion; hence, the hyphenated terms introduced above.

Affinities

The affinities of the Qemant to their neighbors in Ethiopia, an area of 450,000 square miles populated by an estimated 22,000,000 people divided into seventy or more language groups, are of interest. The northern and north-central part of highland Ethiopia, once called Abyssinia, is the region in which field research was conducted. It is inhabited by three major groups which together are sometimes called Abyssinians. They are: the Amhara, who number about 5,000,000 and are politically dominant; the Tegre, numbering about 1,500,000, who are closely related to the Amhara and share political dominance with them; and the Agaw, who are the original inhabitants of most of the region, with a population of about 250,000, and the group to which the Qemant belong. These three peoples are racially one and have many common cultural roots as well, in spite of the fact that the first two groups speak Semitic languages and the third group speaks dialects belonging to the central branch of the Cushitic languages. (Semitic and Cushitic languages constitute two of the five subfamilies of the Afro-Asiatic language family.)

Racially, the vast majority of Ethiopians are Caucasoids. Whether their language is Cushitic or Semitic, they show a common range of somatic characteristics. Some genetic mixture with Negroids (and possibly with Bushmanoids to a very minor degree) has occurred, but the physical features of these latter peoples are not dominant characteristics of most Ethiopians. The Ethiopian Caucasoid is of medium height with a slender to medium build. Skin color ranges from dark brown to a light tan, with the median about midway between the two extremes. A long, narrow head is usual. Noses range from broad to narrow; the medium or narrow nose often has a high bridge. The hair is always black and varies from curly to kinky.

The Agaw and the dominant Amhara and Tegre hold themselves to be superior to Negroids, who live in the lowlands to the west of the Ethiopian high plateau, and they do not intermarry with them, although a man might have children by his Negroid servant. The attitude of the Agaw and Amhara toward people who are somatically different from themselves is summarized by a tale common to both peoples. They say that when God made man, he molded a figurine of clay and fired it; it came from the fire black from overbaking. God then made a second figurine and fired it for a shorter time; this one came out white because it was underfired. Finally, God fired a third figurine which came from the fire a golden brown, that is, an "Ethiopian." He pronounced this one to be perfect and the culmination of His endeavor.

The Semitic-speakers of Ethiopia have a documented history reaching back 1500 years and a less well-recorded history that goes back an additional 1500 years. Before and during the early era of Semitic-speakers, there are dim evidences of sociocultural achievement by the Cushitic-speaking groups of which the Agaw is one.

Today there are eight Agaw groups, remnants of a former much wider distribution of Agaw throughout northern and central Ethiopia. Seven groups—the

Qemant, Awiya, Kumfal, Hamir, Bilan, Damot, and Hamta—are found in enclaves and an eighth—the Falasha—is found dispersed among the Amhara. All Agaw speak either mutually intelligible or nearly mutually intelligible dialects of the Agaw language, and almost all Agaw are bilingual, also speaking Amharic or Tegrenya. Today, however, not all of the Qemant still speak their native Agaw dialect, called Qemantinya. One-third of them speak Qemantinya well; one-third have little knowledge of the dialect and speak Amharic only; and the other third falls in between.

Despite the linguistic change among the Qemant, they preserve, as a group, more of the old Agaw culture and society than any other group, and they are the only ones who retain a pagan-Hebraic religion. Their culture is thus the most distinct from that of the Amhara and Tegre. It was for these reasons that I decided to study the Qemant.

The Qemant long remained culturally distinct and socially semiautonomous from the surrounding, dominant Amhara because their pagan-Hebraic faith provided a barrier which greatly slowed the effects of acculturation.[1] The pagan-Hebraic religion of the Qemant virtually closed their society to outsiders until the 1880s. At that time the Qemant experienced forced acculturation toward the cultural model of the Amhara. This, in turn, effectively ruptured the religious barrier and caused a rapid withering of Qemant culture. Amharization of the Qemant continues into the present, and in its final phase the Qemant sociocultural system is vanishing because of a great decrease of adherents to the old pagan-Hebraic religion, which is intimately tied with the indigenous social structure. Without a necessary minimum of people interacting according to the pagan-Hebraic rules of behavior, Qemant society cannot be perpetuated. Today, the Qemant are on the verge of complete Amharization because this minimum is lacking.

The factors which allowed the Qemant to survive centuries of Amharization, and which may be called boundary-maintaining mechanisms, are examined in this work as they were when still highly effective, until late in the last century. There are still five hundred pagan-Hebraic Qemant and many thousands of partially Amharized "Christian" Qemant. The religious beliefs (and other related cultural patterns in general) of Qemant converted to Christianity vary along a continuum, with Ethiopian Orthodox Christianity at one end and the pagan-Hebraic religion at the other. For convenience, Qemant who have been baptized will here be called "Christian Qemant." A few cultural traits mentioned in this work are no longer observable among the Qemant; these are so identified, and an attempt is made to estimate the time when they disappeared.

This study also examines processes of cultural change affecting the Qemant and their parent Agaw stock. Anthropologists have customarily conducted studies of cultural change as if change did not exist until Europeans appeared on the scene. As Homer Barnett so aptly comments on this matter, "In other words, . . . Euro-American invasion was the outside force which upset the equilibrium

---

[1] For our purpose acculturation is defined as cultural change brought about by the contact of two or more cultures.

that had been reached by peculiarly static indigenous societies and cultures" (1965:216). Apropos of this Ralph Beals had previously written: "It is of the utmost importance that both theoretical and empirical studies give adequate consideration to the reciprocal nature of acculturation and to instances of acculturation which do not involve European cultures" (1953:638). It is noteworthy that the cultural changes discussed in this book were originally reciprocal, among Ethiopian societies, and that European culture played almost no part in them. My account of these reciprocal acculturative changes begins in the following chapter on the culture history of the Agaw.

Previous Visitors

Portuguese clergymen, soldiers, and diplomats visited Ethiopia in the sixteenth and seventeenth centuries. Their narratives often mentioned the Agaw peoples, but did not refer specifically to the Qemant. It is not until the close of the eighteenth century that we begin to learn of the Qemant in the writings of Europeans.

James Bruce, a wealthy Scotsman of immense physical proportions, unveiled the Qemant to the outside world in 1790, and his writings make delightful reading to this day. He gave the West a substantial if somewhat colored introduction to Ethiopia in his *Travels to Discover the Source of the Nile*. Bruce produced five volumes of his adventurous *Travels,* and of these he devoted a little over a page to "the Kemmont . . . a sect once the same as the Falasha . . ." and whose "language is the same as that of the Falasha . . ." (1790,4:275). Bruce wrote that the Qemant were baptized as Christians in the early 1600s by the Emperor Fasil, an Amhara, but that they did not strictly adhere to this faith, "for they retain most of their ancient customs" (1790,4:275). He also noted that the Qemant did not display Christian behavior and they considered the Christians to be "unclean." Bruce's statement regarding baptism of the Qemant at this early time seems to be unwarranted and is not borne out in oral traditions of the Qemant, in traditions and written chronicles of the Amhara, and in narratives of later travelers to Ethiopia. If some Qemant were converted to Christianity in the early 1600s, they were few in number and were most likely those who lived on the outskirts of Fasil's newly built capital of Gondar.

The next European to visit Ethiopia was the Reverend Samuel Gobat, who published in 1834 his *Journal of a Three Years' Residence in Abyssinia,* after returning to England. He believed the "Camaountes" to be monotheists, but noted that when questioned about "their religion, they always answered in an equivocal manner and in the tone of a buffoon" (1834:364). Aside from mentioning that the Qemant have their own priesthood, Gobat learned little more about them than Bruce had. Nevertheless, in the works of Bruce and Gobat we begin to see a theme which recurs in the European narratives, that is, the Qemant hold secret their religion and zealously guard all knowledge concerning it from "unclean" people—anyone not a Qemant.

A German scholar, Eduard Rüppell, who traveled to Ethiopia in the early

1830s, said of the "Gamant," "I could only obtain incomplete notes on their religious opinions" (1840,2:149). These notes covered part of a page and all are included here. Rüppell remarked that the Qemant were pagans, but he also said they were once indigenous "Jews" who had become less Hebraic during the previous centuries of warfare between the Christian and Hebraic peoples of Ethiopia (1840,2:148, 150). Rüppell's remarks touch upon the true nature of Qemant religion; it *is* pagan with some Hebraic religious elements. However, the Qemant did not become less Hebraic through time; they are, and have been for centuries, largely pagan and only slightly Hebraic. This traveler remarked that the Qemant have no special holidays and observe no fasts, both statements of misinformation resulting from the secrecy shrouding the Qemant religion. Rüppell also commented on a rite, including the drinking of beer, that marked the death of a community member.

Our first somewhat substantive account of the "Kamants" comes from a German missionary, Johann Martin Flad, who spent several years in Ethiopia among the Falasha and Qemant. Flad and his German co-workers converted a moderate number of Falasha to Christianity, but they did not have much success in baptizing the Qemant. In fact, the Qemant even misunderstood the nature of a book which the missionaries left with them and I found, almost a century later, hidden in a dark recess of a house in central Qemantland.

The book and the misconception concerning it could easily have remained hidden. However, some Amhara living in Gondar, who were eager to help me with my fieldwork, told me that the Qemant had some mystical and magical books, written in their language. They explained that should I find these writings, I would learn the true nature of the Qemant religion and their world view. It was then my turn to explain to them that the Qemant speak a Cushitic language and no Cushitic language is represented by an indigenous system of writing; therefore, it was not possible for the Qemant to have books written in Qemantinya. In any event, I further explained, ethnographic fieldwork is based upon the fieldworker participating in and observing the behavior of a people during the course of the annual progression of the seasons. Thus by constantly seeing Qemant life and participating in it, as far as possible, I should, within a year, have firmer knowledge of them than I would if I uncovered a "secret book" about them.

The tale of hidden mystical books followed me and was constantly repeated, even by the Qemant who, although an illiterate peasantry, live in awe of writing controlled by the elite and especially in awe of "wonderous books." I invariably squelched these stories by checking all information. Nevertheless, I could not bury the tale, and in one remote reach of Qemantland one person after another claimed to have seen a mystical book in Qemantinya.

Finally, after plying some Qemant with repeated questions and drinks, I was lead to a house where a carefully wrapped packet was taken from its hiding place. Thereupon the Qemant unwrapped the packet and handed to me a musty 5- by 8-inch pamphlet. While the illiterate peasants and priests surrounding me beamed with "I-told-you-so" looks and chatted about the powerful religious writings in this "sacred book," I read the title: *An Adara Yasus Krestos qadasaw wangal safaw sana qadasaw Marqos* (literally, in Qemantinya: I, God, Jesus Christ's

Holy Gospel according to St. Mark). The book, and there must be others like it hidden in Qemantland, was a missionary pamphlet translated from German to the Agaw dialect of the Qemant and Falasha by associates of Flad. The pamphlet was produced in Vienna by a printer who possessed type in the Geez syllabary of over 280 characters, used for all writing by the literate elite of Ethiopia.

While among the Qemant, Flad noted the taboo they have against women during menstruation, the existence of the "higher priests" in their religion, and the ceremonies they hold in sacred groves of trees, as well as a few points concerning their rituals (1866:18–21). Flad seems to have believed, at least in part, some wild tales about the Qemant—that they were incestuous and "that they never let a person die a natural death, but if any of their relatives is near expiring, the priest of the village is called to cut his throat . . ." (1866:18–19). However, Flad realized that "the Kamants being so very reluctant to let any thing be seen or heard of their religious observances may have given rise to such monstrous accusations" (1866:19). Our missionary writer again calls our attention to the difficulty in learning anything about the Qemant, and especially about their religion. In the same vein, Henry Stern, a missionary contemporary of Flad's who could not pry much religious information from the Qemant either, commented that they "had so little to communicate." He did note, however, that "at stated times, [they] repair to certain rocks to perform secret acts of devotion . . ." (1862:43).

Another German traveler in Ethiopia, Martin von Heuglin, introduces the Qemant as pagans who are "feared by Christians as thieves and highwaymen" and notes that they are not interested in contact with strangers. Von Heuglin also observed close sociopolitical bonds existing between the Qemant peasantry and the Amhara elite—bonds recounted in Qemant oral traditions. The German traveler says: "The Gamants, because of their faithfulness and bravery to the Emperor, are very much valued and are for the most part special retainers of his family . . ." (1868:256).

This close political and military cooperation between the Qemant and the Amhara elite allowed the latter to build their first permanent capital, during the 1630s, inside of Qemantland. The Qemant vassals apparently knew their place politically, despite what the average Christian Amhara thought about their conduct. Therefore, the Amhara monarchs could place more trust in their Qemant vassals than they could in Amhara and Tegre nobility and peasants who could aspire to regional political autonomy or even national political control. This alliance of the Qemant and the Amhara is a major factor contributing to the survival of the Qemant's pagan-Hebraic religion during centuries of bloody warfare between the Christian Amhara and other Hebraic Agaw peoples, who were steadily crushed as time went on. The Qemant were insured for a time against peaceful Amharization by the survival of their religion, the focal point of internal cultural factors inhibiting acculturative change among them.

Hormuzd Rassam, a member of the British Mission in the 1860s to Emperor Theodore of Ethiopia, also says, "No King of Abyssinia ever had such loyal subjects as these Kamants have proved themselves by their devotion to Theodore . . ." (1869, 1:209). Noting that the Qemant often hold their rites in groves of trees "regarded as sacred," Rassam says, "Their religion is as great a mystery in Abyssinia as that of the Ansairies is in Syria, and . . . they still continue to practice certain rites and ceremonies unknown to either Christians or Mussulmans" (1869, 1:209).

Almost 200 years of the above fleeting glimpses of the Qemant by Europeans were brought together by the American geographer Frederick Simoons, who added in 1953–1954 to the previous knowledge with his own fieldwork among the peoples of Bagemder and Semen, the province in which the Qemant reside. As I shall explain, it was his interesting study, *Northwest Ethiopia* (1960), that was *actually* the magical book in my fieldwork among the Qemant.

It is often difficult for an anthropologist to convey to the people he studies his reason for conducting fieldwork. This is especially true among peasants, such as the Qemant, who have been almost unexposed to Western influence. They are suspicious of strangers and their motives and particularly distrustful of written endeavor, an art they cannot participate in or examine. It should be remembered that the Qemant are controlled in part by the written word used by the Amhara elite to which these peasants are subordinate.

The elite has a tradition of writing historical manuscripts—hand-lettered works usually stored in religious buildings. Therefore, I was able to explain to the Qemant and their Amhara and Falasha neighbors that I was writing a book on the history of the Qemant, including their present way of life. While they contemplated this statement, I produced Simoons' book as an example of similar work done by a European. When they opened the book, each person's eyes were immediately riveted on the photographs of Qemant, Falasha, and Amhara in familiar surroundings. Of course many of them recognized pictures of themselves or acquaintances. Simoons' photography was proof that there was a precedent for work similar to mine in which the life ways of a local people had been studied and recorded in a book. Furthermore, as everyone knew quite well, no harm had befallen these people. Finally, the photographs held the exhilarating possibility that any informant might also appear in a wonderous book. Such are the ways of the strange and inscutable Europeans!

Before discovering who the Qemant are, a people described by Simoons as "secretive about their beliefs and rituals" (1960:39), and seeing how they earn their daily bread and what their life is as it unfolds from day to day, we look into the historical backgrounds of the Qemant and their Agaw ancestors.

2

The Dynamics of Agaw Culture History

A BRIEF, INTRODUCTORY OUTLINE of Agaw culture history is presented here to provide historical context for the Qemant division of the Agaw peoples. Relatively little is known of Ethiopia's past. There are few comprehensive works on Ethiopian prehistory and history, and none have shown fully the central role which the Agaw have played.

Prehistory

By 5000 B.C., and probably well before, Bushmanoid and Caucasoid hunters and gatherers occupied the Ethiopian Plateau and surrounding areas. The Caucasoid hunters and gatherers undoubtedly were the ancestors of the Cushitic-speaking peoples of present-day Ethiopia, including the Qemant.

Botanical evidence indicates that Ethiopia was an ancient center of plant domestication and dispersal, but not a wholly independent center of plant domestication. It is not the Bushmanoids, but the ancestral Cushitic-speakers who are responsible for this early agricultural center. From the present distribution of Agaw enclaves in north and central Ethiopia, we infer that their ancestors were the original Cushitic-speaking population of this area. The ancestral Agaw cultivated varieties of plants, including wheat and barley, that reached them by diffusion, domesticated certain local plants such as the small-grained *tef,* the oil seed *nug,* and perhaps finger millet, and preserved archaic domesticated plants such as lintless flax, cultivated only as an oil seed. Horticultural techniques and plants, such as wheat, barley, and flax, came around 3000 B.C. to the ancestral Agaw, who were in a direct spatial line of diffusion from the Middle Eastern agricultural center. Animal husbandry came from Nubia around 2000 B.C. or earlier.

The horticultural technology of the Ethiopian Caucasoids gave them a cultural advantage over Bushmanoids, allowing greater population growth and density, more efficient use of the physical environment, and increased leisure for various pursuits, one of which was group organization for warfare. Bushmanoids were thus displaced and perhaps absorbed to some degree.

By the beginning of the first millennium B.C., Cushitic-speaking peoples dominated Ethiopia and expanded into adjacent areas to the south, in what is now Kenya, Uganda, and Tanzania. This was just before southern Arabians and their culture moved into the northern part of the Agaw area.

The Ethiopic Civilization

By the end of the second millennium B.C., a civilization based economically on irrigated crops had developed in the relatively well-watered highlands of Yemen. Sometime after 1000 B.C. small groups of people from the southern Arabian states began to colonize the highlands of Ethiopia in the area north of the Takaze River. This colonization continued for many centuries, perhaps for a millennium or more. The indigenous people with whom the southern Arabians came into contact were the ancestral Agaw.

In the area of contact, fusion of the southern Arabian culture and the ancestral Agaw culture resulted in a third culture. Fusion did not entirely obliterate the originally distinct cultural traits, and southern Arabian elements were predominant. A level of sociocultural development that is suitably called civilization began in Ethiopia as the fusion took place, and it is appropriate to use the name "Ethiopic Civilization" for this blended culture. At this time, and in this way, Ethiopia became the southernmost march of civilization in Africa.

The southern Arabians made numerous contributions to the Ethiopic Civilization. They introduced technological elements such as dry stone masonry, monumental architecture, irrigation associated with terracing of hillsides, and perhaps iron and the plow. More complex forms of social organization were also introduced by the southern Arabians. The most basic form was the dual structure, introduced in the first chapter, of an urban elite with its Great Tradition, and a rural peasantry with its Little Tradition. Writing was perhaps the most important of the new cultural elements brought to Ethiopia by the southern Arabians. Although the colonists from southern Arabia were few, their language or, more specifically its successor (called Ethiopic or Geez) became linguistically dominant.

The ancestral Agaw also made many contributions to the Ethiopic Civilization. Because they supplied the bulk of the population, they determined the somatic characteristics of the Ethiopic people. In addition, they furnished some linguistic elements. Furthermore, the ancestral Agaw provided the basic crops of the Ethiopic agricultural civilization, not only those such as wheat and barley, already known in southern Arabia, but many indigenous crops as well.

Throughout the centuries, there were several centers of Ethiopic Civilization. Its last florescence focused on Aksum, a monumental religious center dating from around the beginning of the Christian era. Hebraic religious elements had diffused earlier to Ethiopia from southern Arabia, but Christianity reached Ethiopia in the fourth century during the reign of Ezana of the Ethiopic

Aksumite state. Christianity took hold slowly in Aksum, spreading first among the urban elite, and later drifting down to the Ethiopic peasantry.

Ethiopic Civilization began to wane near the end of the sixth century, when it lost to Persia possessions it had earlier gained in southern Arabia. Islamic expansion blocked access to the Mediterranean, Arabian, and East African centers with which the Ethiopic people had traded. During the eighth century, the Beja, a Northern Cushitic-speaking group, invaded Aksum and severed its connection to the Christian states in Nubia, the remaining link with the outside world. The final blow to the waning Ethiopic Civilization was a reaction to Ethiopic culture by some of the Agaw peoples. This process will be explained in a following subsection. Edward Gibbon depicted the state of affairs well in saying, "Encompassed on all sides by the enemies of their religion, the Ethiopians slept near a thousand years, forgetful of the world, by whom they were forgotten."

The Southward Movement of Ethiopic Civilization

The Ethiopic Civilization atrophied, but it did not perish. Surrounded by the Beja and Islamic forces, most of the residual Ethiopic Civilization concentrated its remaining energies toward the interior of the Ethiopian Plateau. Sometime before A.D. 900, part of the Ethiopic people pushed into the territory of the Agaw south of the Takaze River. A process of fusion then resulted from the long-term contact between the Agaw and the Ethiopic migrants. (Since the Ethiopic migrants are the predominant of the two ancestral strains of the present-day Amhara, they will hereafter be called proto-Amhara.) The Ethiopic people who remained north of the Takaze River are the ancestors of the present-day Tegre.

The primitive Agaw south of the Takaze were subordinated by military power as an emerging peasantry under the proto-Amhara elite with its Great Tradition and alongside the proto-Amhara peasantry with its Little Tradition. The inclusion of the Agaw south of the Takaze in proto-Amhara society provided the social matrix within which acculturation took place. This is an example of social change preceding, and providing a basis for, cultural change. After many centuries of culture contact the proto-Amhara and most of the Agaw merged, via a process of fusion, and a third cultural system emerged—the Amhara proper. Several Agaw groups, including the Qemant, remained culturally distinct and did not lose their identity in the growing population of the Amhara.

Although the acculturation process was reciprocal, the proto-Amhara elements predominated. As a result, the Amharic language is Semitic, but has strong Agaw characteristics; the religion of the Amhara proper is Christian, but includes many pagan and Hebraic Agaw elements; and the agriculture of the Amhara is dominated by crops developed by the Agaw. Although the proto-Amhara culture had received some cultural elements of the Agaw through the earlier fusion of the ancestral Agaw and southern Arabian colonists, many elements entered or were reinforced through the secondary fusion.

The technology and organization of the proto-Amhara opened up resources of the physical environment which the Agaw south of the Takaze previously were not able to exploit. With the introduction of the iron-tipped plow, other iron tools, and additional agricultural techniques, more land was put under cultivation. By "plowing" deep furrows, the Agaw could either drain the fields in seasonally marshy areas or irrigate the fields in unseasonally dry periods. These are but two examples of various techniques which enabled the Agaw to produce more food than formerly. The technological change and intensified economic development led to an increase of population. In turn, more people cleared and turned over more land, causing the forests of the central part of the Ethiopian Plateau to dwindle. Without the cover of the forest and swamp areas, the game upon which Agaw horticulturalists had been partially dependent disappeared. Hence, proto-Amhara technology also closed part of the physical environment and its resources and prevented the Agaw from returning to their old ways. Thus, in the course of acculturation the occupational role of the Agaw was changed from that of primitive horticulturalist and hunter to that of peasant agriculturalist.

The Agaw Reaction to Culture Contact

Indigenous groups respond to contact imposed by a more powerful group. The process may take a passive form, in which the first group withdraws into enclaves, or, the process may take a more reactive form in which the people imposed upon participate in a nativistic or revitalization movement that may return this group to power and independence. The intrusion of the proto-Amhara provoked a nativistic movement among those Agaw south of the Takaze, who were partially acculturated or unacculturated. The movement spread and was the final blow given to the atrophied center of Ethiopic Civilization north of the Takaze River. The legendary Queen Yehudit (Judith) of the Falasha Agaw may have been among the Agaw chiefs who reacted militarily against the Amhara-Tegre power from perhaps the ninth through the eleventh centuries.

Historical records do not make it clear when the Agaw became the monarchs of a large part of old Abyssinia. However, it is fairly certain that the Zagwe Dynasty of the Agaw of Lasta formally held political power in Abyssinia from A.D. 1137 to 1270. At this time Abyssinia was a polity which included the northern and the central part of the Ethiopian Plateau. Indications, from Ethiopian manuscripts and oral traditions, that the Agaw assumed political power earlier may reflect the repeated waxing and waning of Amhara-Tegre power during the Agaw reaction.

While the Agaw were in political control, the marginal civilization of the Amhara and Tegre entered what has been called a "dark age," of which we know very little. Economic depression probably reached its nadir, and large-scale marketing came to an end. Markets then were found only in or near villages or in open rural areas rather than in towns. Urban centers became uninhabitable ruins. The Amhara-Tegre Great Tradition became totally rural and became less differentiated from the Little Traditions of the masses of peasants and emergent peasants, especially in the spheres of material goods and technology. Internal and external communication was greatly disrupted, often almost at a standstill, and regionalism prevailed. A large part of the heritage of the Ethiopic Civilization was lost or destroyed at this time.

The Emergence of the Abyssinian Feudal State

The Amhara took control of medieval Abyssinia around A.D. 1270 following a revolt against the Zagwe Dynasty in which the last Agaw ruler of Abyssinia was killed. This successful revolt returned political control of the country to the heirs of the Ethiopic tradition and marked the beginning of the medieval Abyssinian feudal state. The feudal state had its roots in the Dark Ages, thrived in the Middle Ages, and continued until the emergence of the present Ethiopian state during the 1890s.

Improved bureaucratic organization, communication, and military technology would have been necessary to support a sedentary, urban-centered royal court. Such improvement was impossible in the impoverished and encircled country. Therefore, in order to minimize the forces of regionalism, which would have fragmented Abyssinia, the royal court became a wandering military camp. As in Europe, a feudal organization of men and land was necessary to continue a semblance of a nation-state and to distribute goods and services throughout the land. Cooperation between religious and political administrators increased, with the Church and the state supporting one another.

During the Agaw reaction to Amhara power, Amhara culture was not entirely rejected. Christianity, the prestigious religion of civilization, grew, and the process of fusion continued at a diminished rate. Christianity, as practiced by both Agaw and Amhara, incorporated many of the older pagan and Hebraic elements, and this partially accounts for its rapid spread. The process of fusion accelerated after Amhara power was restored, and most of the remaining Agaw were again subordinated as a peasantry to the Amhara feudal elite. In certain areas acculturation was slow, and some Agaw groups like the Qemant became enclaves within the expanding Amhara population. As a result, some Agaw experienced regional stabilized pluralism (arrested fusion), retaining their own unique Little Tradition under the dominant Amhara. Most of these pockets of Agaw, except the Qemant, continued to resist the Amhara, often with arms, during the next four centuries.

As the Middle Ages progressed, the Amhara proper became a large majority of the population. The earlier process of fusion had been possible because of the large size of the Agaw population, but the influence of the Agaw waned as their numbers dwindled. Acculturation gradually changed from fusion of Amhara and Agaw to assimilation of the Agaw by the Amhara. This assimilative acculturation will be called "Amharization," a process of change which emerged by the end of the fifteenth century.

The high plateau of Abyssinia was invaded by the Muslims in 1527 and later by the Galla, an East Cushitic-speaking people. In addition, the Amhara were occupied with constant military action against enclaves of unacculturated Agaw. After Amhara power was reestablished in the thirteenth century Abyssinia had begun contact with the West. The maritime technology nurtured by Prince Henry the Navigator allowed the Portuguese, spurred by their crusading spirit, to begin and maintain continuous contact with Abyssinia. Military aid arrived from Portugal in 1540 and helped end the Muslim invasion which had devastated Abyssinia. The Portuguese introduced firearms, with which the Amhara feudal elite finally suppressed Agaw revolts and preserved the frontiers against Islam. The Galla within Amhara territory were brought within the feudal structure and many were eventually assimilated into the Amhara culture. In the 1630s the Abyssinian feudal elite rejected Portuguese influence because the Jesuits had caused civil strife with a controversy between their Roman rite and Abyssinia's Alexandrian rite.

Modern Ethiopia

In the 1630s a permanent capital was constructed at Gondar, inside the Qemant area. The Portuguese had supplied architectural and engineering aid for this project before their expulsion. It was possible to build Gondar, the first urban center since Aksum, because the Amhara were in complete political control of the Qemant, a group which never constituted serious opposition to the Amhara feudal organization. Gondar remained the capital until the 1850s.

In the 1870s and 1880s Emperor Johannes IV defended Abyssinia against Egypt and then against the Dervishes of the Mahdi in the Sudan. Emperor Menelik II (1889–1913) turned back European intrusion at the battle of Adwa (1896), in which the Italians were defeated and their plans for colonization were shattered. Menelik II established the capital at Addis Ababa, conquered lands to the south of Abyssinia, and introduced elements of Western industrial urban technology. Under Menelik's reign, Abyssinia was transformed and expanded into a larger, more modern nation named Ethiopia.

Change in Ethiopia continues at a faster rate under the present Emperor, Haile Sellassie I. Ethiopia experienced occupation by mechanized Italian military forces from 1936 to 1941, in the early years of the Emperor's reign. Today, bureaucratic modernization and an enlarging program of public education are aiding the growth of various nuclei of industrial-urbanization which eventually will transform Ethiopia into a powerful state.

3

The Qemant Communities
and Their Setting

THE QEMANT COMMUNITIES visited and studied during the course of the fieldwork are not only related to one another but to those of the dominant Amhara, who surround them. To illustrate this point, Qemant ties with the national Amhara society are examined in this chapter, and an account of the Qemant communities, homesteads, and religious sites follows. For a clearer picture of Qemantland, the regional environmental setting is explored first.

Physical Environment

Ethiopia has several distinct physiographic divisions, each with its own climate. The most important of these divisions is the Ethiopian Plateau, which is oval in plan, extending about 900 miles from the northern to the southern border of the western half of Ethiopia. From east to west, it measures about 500 miles across at its widest point. Averaging 7000 feet above sea level, the plateau is bounded by steep escarpments on all sides, except along Ethiopia's southern border, where it tapers off into moderately rugged terrain. Savanna, that becomes a morass in the rainy season, desert, and steppe surround most of the escarpment like a moat about a castle. Plains, ranges of hills, and mountainlike remnants of table lands make up the surface of the plateau, which is cut by several major canyons, such as those of the Blue Nile and Takaze, by many other rivers, and hundreds of lesser streams. Thirty to eighty inches of rain fall on various parts of the plateau each year. The precipitation is very heavy from June to October.

The rugged and dissected terrain, the rampartlike escarpments, and the torrential inundations of the Ethiopian Plateau have long hindered external and internal communication. These geographical barriers have impeded cultural diffusion to the plateau from the outside and within the plateau by invasion, migration, or any other means. These physical obstacles have been major factors contributing to Ethiopia's long political independence, its history of regional political autonomy, and the differentiation and preservation of societies and cultures on the Ethiopian Plateau. To be sure, peoples and culture traits have penetrated these barriers and traversed the high plateau for millennia, but the barriers have discouraged cultural diffusion.

Qemantland, a somewhat rugged part of the northwestern region of the plateau lying 18 miles to the north of Lake Tana, varies in altitude from 4000 to over 10,000 feet. Irregular in shape, it measures approximately 30 miles by 50 miles.

Qemant traditions state that their land was forested in the times of the first Qemant, but their region now appears somewhat brown and barren in the dry season after all the crops have been harvested. This is because much of the tree cover has been removed through centuries of intensive agriculture. Nevertheless, varieties of acacia, juniper, cedar, wild fig, candelabra euphorbia, and aloes sporadically dot the landscape. Occasionally, one finds a natural stand of timber, spared only because the area is untillable or the site is ritually protected for worship. A few lowland areas have more widespread stretches of trees, usually varieties of acacia. Australian eucalypti, introduced around the turn of the century, are grown for construction purposes and are found, in stands of twenty or more trees, around some of the homesteads.

Powerful, sharp-eyed kites stretch their great, red wings as they soar above the heights of the Qemant homeland. Now and then they swoop down into valleys in search of food, sometimes seizing a rodent or a hare in their talons. At other times, these members of the eagle family compete with vultures for carrion. Smaller birds, often colored in bright hues of red, yellow, or iridescent blue-green, glide through the trees and dart across the fields.

Large, wild mammals are not found in Qemantland, except in the lowest and most western reaches. Many uncultivated areas support dik-diks, small antelope about a foot high with a coat that looks and feels like steel wool. Medium-sized antelope, wildcats, anteaters, bush pigs, and spotted hyenas are now rather infrequent in most of Qemantland. One of the world's rarest game animals, a wild mountain goat known as the walia, is said to still live in the highest and most rugged parts of the Qemant highland.

Monkeys are the most predominant wild mammals in the Qemant area. One is also more apt to find a dead monkey than any other kind of animal, because most Qemant attempt to kill them by throwing well-aimed stones. "Monkeys destroy our crops and we destroy them," the Qemant remark.

Monkeys in Qemantland are of three varieties. The arboreal and vegetarian Colobinae are exemplified by the eye-catching black and white Colobus monkey with its long silky fur and bushy tail. Since it is confined exclusively to the trees, and groves of trees are rare, the Colobus is not seen frequently. Much more common is an arboreal and omniverous Cercopithecinae, the grayish Grivet monkey which sports white tufts of hair on the sides of its black face. The Grivet is far more adaptive than the Colobus, surviving in part by pillaging crops in places where there are only a few trees because the peasants have cleared the land. A terrestrial Cercopithecinae, the olive baboon, makes his home in the lowland areas where the terrain is not completely cultivated. Many troops contain males far larger than

Plowing the rocky soil of Qemantland in the dry season.

any peasant's dog. Qemant do not stone the baboons; instead, they try to avoid their defensively formidable groups.

A species of otter frequents the water courses, which are filled with fingerlings during the dry season and support fish a foot or two in length during the rainy season, when streams are swollen. The fish, mainly Nile perch, swim up the full streams from Lake Tana, apparently to lay their eggs, and then leave Qemantland, returning to the lake at the end of the rainy season.

Although the surface of Qemantland is stoney and rugged in most areas, the soil, often of volcanic origin, is quite fertile. The mild weather and the 50 inches of rain which fall between April and October provide excellent conditions for agriculture. There are two rainy seasons. The "little rains," which are light showers, usually fall in April, but may fall anytime from February through mid-May. Some years there are only traces of the little rains. May and early June are usually dry. After the two dry months, the "big rains" make a deluge from July through September. The mean annual temperature in most of Qemantland ranges from 60 to 70°, making it a realm of eternal spring.

During the big rains, the sluggish streams of the dry season rise, and the soil is churned into mud. Internal communication in the Qemant area then virtually sloshes to a halt. Reflecting these circumstances, the ceremonial calendar of the pagan-Hebraic Qemant includes no regularly scheduled religious observances during the big rains. At this time the skies are dark much of the time, and the hills, valleys, and water courses are a dreary brown. Toward the middle of the rainy season the crops and the natural grass cover begin to sprout, and by late September the skies are sunny and the landscape is verdant. Communication is then restored and the harvest follows. As the dry season progresses after September, the countryside fades eventually to a dusty reddish-brown, perhaps to be revived by the little rains.

The ecological zones of the Qemant area are also found throughout much of the Ethiopian Plateau. These zones are best explained by the Ethiopians' own system of categorization as follows:

1. *Qolla.* Ranging from sea level to 7000 feet. Warm to hot climate; often disease ridden. Some parts are humid during the big rains. Characteristic crops are white *tef* (an important cereal with grains the size of fine sand and indigenous to northern and central Ethiopia), sorghums, cotton, and finger millet.
   a. *Baraha.* Lowest and hottest of the *qolla.* Said to have spontaneous grass and forest fires, and thought to be excessively unhealthy.
   b. *Medera bada* (land with nothing). Driest of the *qolla.* Refers to true desert, whereas *baraha* is semidesert.
2. *Wayna dega.* Ranging from 6000 to 9000 feet. Temperate climate. Characteristic crops are red *tef,* wheat, barley, and peas.
3. *Dega.* Ranging from 8000 to 15,000 feet. Cool to cold zone. Barley is the principal *dega* crop, but lentils, edible flax, and broad beans will also grow, although frost kills them in certain years. *Chowqe,* ranging from 12,000 to 15,000 feet, is the coldest and highest projections of the *dega.* Descriptive of the uninhabited higher mountain slopes, such as Ras Dajan and Guna. No farming and little grazing is done here.

Elevations given above are approximate and serve only as a guide since the zones are not demarcated exclusively by altitude but also by climate, crops, and especially by opinion. Thus, a person from the *dega* will call an area *qolla* that others call *wayna dega* because it is warmer than the climate of the area to which he is accustomed. Both *wayna dega* and *dega* dwellers think their own zone to be the best in which to live. It was not definitely learned whether *qolla* dwellers think their ecological zone to be the "best of all possible worlds," although some so stated. Most of the Qemant live in *wayna dega,* and some in *dega* and higher *qolla.*

Ties between the Qemant and Ethiopia

The Qemant peasant communities were integrated into first the Abyssinian and later the Ethiopian nation by administrative and economic bonds, and thus their ties with the nation are ancient. An Amhara-Tegre feudal elite today controls and taxes the Qemant, as it does all of the ethnic groups of the nation.

The vehicular track from Azazo to Chelga, in foreground and as a white line in the midground, as it crosses a more desolate part of Qemantland in the Guwang valley. The area in the photograph is qolla.

This feudal structure is gradually being transformed into a modern bureaucracy on the industrial-urban model, but at present the Qemant, who are in a lower stratum of the feudal structure, are still in direct contact with feudal administrators. Lower-level administrative positions in Qemant areas are often filled by Qemant who either have been Amharized or have demonstrated a strong allegiance to the Amhara on the battlefield or otherwise.

Ethiopia has five levels of governmental administration: (1) the nation or Empire, (2) the province or Governor Generalate (*tekelay gazat*), (3) the subprovince (*awraja*), (4) the sub-subprovince (*warada*), and (5) the sub-sub-subprovince (*meketel warada*). Gondar, the imperial capital until the 1850s, is now the capital of Bagemder and Semen Governor Generalate and is an administrative, market, religious, and educational center of about 13,000 people. Gondar is connected with other major towns and cities of Ethiopia by air and by a gravel road running north and south.

The Qemant enclave is divided by the Guwang River into eastern and western halves. There is a slight difference in speech, terminology for certain cultural elements, and ceremonial practice between these two halves. This cleavage was recognized by the Qemant politicoreligious organization, by the Amhara feudal organization which succeeded it, and by the modern Ethiopian subprovincial boundaries. One-half of the Qemant are in the Gondar *awraja*, which is administered from the town of Gondar, and the other half are in the Chelga *awraja*, which is administered from the village of Aykel, near the eastern boundary of this *awraja*.

Economic bonds are created by the regional market system under which the small surplus of agricultural products of the Qemant peasantry is traded in local markets and in the huge Gondar market. Qemant communities near Gondar, such as Karkar, conduct more trade in the Gondar market than do more distant Qemant communities such as Chelga. In the last thirty years, part of the surplus products entering the Gondar market has been shipped outside the province. Such shipments are destined for other major Ethiopian markets, where they are consumed or sold into the world market.

Since the beginning of a more advanced phase of Amharization at the end of the last century, a third factor has begun to knit an increasing number of Qemant into the national fabric. This is the organization of the all-powerful Ethiopian Orthodox Church, whose priests and churches are now found in all Qemant communities.

The Communities

The present study, it will be recalled, is based on fieldwork done principally in two Qemant communities, Karkar and Chelga. Aside from their importance as pagan-Hebraic religious and political centers, they are indistinguishable from other Qemant communities. The Karkar community is considered to be in the *wayna dega,* but has *dega* and *qolla* communities to its north. The community of Chelga includes both *wayna dega* and *qolla* in its area. The Italians have measured a high part of Karkar as 8873 feet above sea level and a low part as 6500 feet. Their measurement for a high part of Chelga is 6732 feet (Consociazione Turistica Italiana 1938:232, 362).

As previously mentioned, all Qemant live in dispersed settlements, and the Qemant of Karkar and Chelga are no exception. Homesteads consisting of single houses or clusters of two to four houses are located anywhere from 300 to 3000 feet from other homesteads. Clusters of ten to twenty houses are rare among the Qemant, and villages, as defined by George P. Murdock, do not exist. In Murdock's terms (1949:80), the Qemant community is a *"neighborhood,* with its families scattered in semi-isolated homesteads," as opposed to a *"village . . .* a concentrated cluster of dwellings near the center of the exploited territory." Karkar and Chelga, like other Qemant neighborhoods, have a mosaic pattern of cultivated fields, fallow land, pasture, and brush, interspersed with "indigenous" houses, which are either oval or circular and have wattle-and-daub walls and thatch roofs. There are usually no large stretches of unoccupied land between the communities.

Artificial and natural boundaries differentiate one community from another. The communities of the Qemant are defined by their own traditions, and do not completely coincide with the recently established Christian parishes and governmental administrative units. The most significant bond of cohesion for a community of pagan-Hebraic Qemant is mutual participation in religious ceremonies.

A detailed study was made of the community of Karkar, which is divided into three subcommunities by a range of hills and an escarpment. One of these three segments, called Karkar Anchaw Mikael, was the actual site of the fieldwork. This segment of Karkar owes its importance to the fact that it contains a pass connecting the drainage basins of the Blue Nile and the Takaze. Through it runs a centuries-old and important route to Gondar. The population of this segment in 1965 was 650, while the population of "greater" Karkar was 2640.

The southeastern point of the Karkar triangle lies a little over 6 miles by road and vehicular track from the outskirts of Gondar (see frontispiece map). The track was cut during the Italian occupation. However, it had not been used since until the arrival of my vehicle, a Volkswagon "bug" which was sometimes pushed and carried in places where locomotion was impossible. The track runs about two-and-one-half miles due west from the road and terminates about one-fourth of the way into Karkar Anchaw Mikael. Another track cut by the Italians, later abandoned, and reopened during the 1965 dry season, runs 12 miles northwest from the eastern end of the first track to the northern tip of the Karkar triangle. Despite the existence of the tracks, communication and transportation from Karkar to Gondar and other areas are still entirely by foot, donkey, or mule.

The lowest level of administration in Karkar, which constitutes two-thirds of Karkar-Walaj *meketel warada,* is conducted by Qemant and Amhara feudal officials, who reside there. The officials on the higher levels of *warada* and *awraja* are in Gondar town.

Chelga, the community of my secondary study, is somewhat larger in population than Karkar. Chelga's center is 6 miles to the south of Gondar by the road and 35 miles by vehicular track to the west across the Guwang River. During the past few years, government-owned Land Rovers and jeeps and a truck belonging to a merchant have plied this track when the rivers were low. The boundaries of the Qemant community of Chelga coincide roughly with those of the Chelga *meketel warada.* Two villages, which serve as administrative and market centers for the Chelga *warada* and the Chelga *awraja,* are found within the confines of the community or neighborhood of Chelga. Both of these villages are inhabited largely by non-Qemant, are of recent origin, and are mentioned here to give a complete picture of the community of Chelga. The use of the label "Chelga" for administrative units larger than the original Qemant community is a recent Amhara practice.

Aykel, the larger of the two villages, is the administrative center for Chelga *awraja.* It is thirty-five years old and has a population of about 800. Within its governmental compound (*gibi*) are several stone buildings of an old Amhara style. Most of the houses of "indigenous style" have been or are being replaced by houses of "new style" which have wattle-and-daub walls, tin roofs, and are rectangular. The new-style buildings include several drinking houses, one eating house, and several merchants' shops in addition to a small elementary school and telephone house for a new line to Gondar. Saraba, the smaller village, serves as the administrative center for Chelga *warada,* and has a population of about one hundred. It is about twenty years old and consists of a large cluster of indigenous houses to which some new-style houses and a modern concrete primary school are added.

Tekel Denga, a recent marketing and administrative village north of Karkar, also has several new-style structures. Aykel, Saraba, and Tekel Denga are the only villages of any kind within the Qemant area and are not native to it. New-style houses are extremely rare outside of these three villages, and the Qemant had none until 1961.

A center for the national Ministry of Community Development lies between Aykel and Saraba. Aside from the primary school in Saraba, the center is the only structure in the Qemant area that is built on a Western architectural design with industrially manufactured materials, other than roofing tin.

The Homestead

Gray-haired Erada, an iron-muscled plowman of sixty, is the head of a typical Qemant homestead. About 1000 feet distant is the homestead of his younger brother, Ayo. In Erada's house live his cheerful, almost-plump wife, Adonech, who is fifty years of age, and slender and unmarried Malke, who is twenty years of age and the youngest of their three sons. Aynaw, the frail and ailing eighty-five-year-old father of Erada, also resides in the house. Robust Nagash and Bitaw, thirty-five and thirty years of age, respectively, are Erada's two married sons; each lives in his own house adjacent to his father's dwelling. Situated in the midst of cultivated fields, these three closely spaced houses and several smaller structures constitute Erada's homestead.

Like other indigenous Qemant houses, those of Erada's homestead have wattle-and-daub walls and thatch roofs and are of two shapes; the more common in Qemantland is oval and the less common is circular. The dwellings of Erada and of Bitaw are oval and average 15 by 24 feet, and the third, a circular house belonging to Nagash, is about 22 feet in diameter. Two center poles are used in the oval plan, whereas the circular plan has either a single center pole or, in larger houses, a set of four or more center poles implanted in a circular pattern between the center and the wall. The circular house has a pointed conical roof and the oval house has a roof that is oval at its base and projects upward to an oval apex nearly 3 feet long. For light and ventilation, both houses have a single wooden door attached to a vertical wooden pivot beam. A circular stone with a hole in its center is often implanted in the ground to receive the bottom of the sharpened beam.

Erada and other Qemant say that the oval plan has always been more popular because "it has more room" and because the two center poles divide the house into thirds. The third nearest the door is used by Erada and Adonech for entertaining, handicrafts, meals, and sleeping, and contains their general hearth. Smoke from the hearth, which consists of three stones, filters up through the thatch roof, coated with a sooty accumulation. The central third of the house is used mainly for storage, being filled with tall segmented storage cylinders, 5 feet high, made of mud and dung. The two thirds nearest the door are called *walal*. The dark third in the rear, called *majat,* is Adonech's "kitchen," where another hearth is located and where she brews beer. Except for food and coffee for guests, food for the family is prepared here by Adonech so that neighbors may not see the amounts and kinds of food consumed.

An elder, with rifle over his shoulder, and his wife and some of their grandchildren outside of their house, one of the few in Qemantland with a stone and earthen wall.

Household furniture and fixtures include beds, chairs, and elongated chairs or "sofas" made of frames of boughs of trees crossed with strips of leather. Furniture is made at home by Erada and his sons. Some houses have an earthen bench built into the wall for use in sitting and sleeping. A large wooden mortar (about 3 feet high by 1½ feet in diameter) and pestle and an earthen platform in which a grinding stone is set are found in every house. Both the mortar and pestle and the platform, a variety of saddle quern, are used by Adonech and the wives of her sons in pounding and grinding cereals, oil seeds, and legumes. The pride of each household is a *masob,* a basket with a pedestal for the serving and storage of food. This one-piece basket has a separate conical cover fitting over its flat top where the food is kept. Elaborate meals and food served to guests are consumed while sitting around this basket. A wooden box or two, many baskets made by Adonech and her daughters-in-law, pots made by the Falasha, and a few gourds complete the list of household fixtures and furnishings, excluding clothing, tools, and weapons.

Erada's homestead, like others, has one or more cylindrical huts with undaubed wattle walls and thatch roofs for goats and donkeys, and particularly for young animals of all species raised. Older animals, especially cattle and sometimes horses and mules, are kept in a nearby corral made of tree boughs and thorn brush. Chickens roost in the main house, and many people keep donkeys and other animals in the house at night. Each dwelling has an adjoining granary, which may be a cylindrical structure placed on stilts, with wattle-and-daub walls and thatch roof, or a cylindrical subterranean pit located outside the house. One-man sleeping huts for mature, unmarried sons are common. They are small, rectangular, and constructed from the same materials as the houses. Malke sleeps in one of these just outside his father's house and next to those once used by his two brothers. A small, fenced garden for vegetables and spices adjoins the homestead, and the main fields for grain, oil seeds, and pulses are separated plots at various distances from the dwellings. Therefore, all fields controlled by a family are not unified into one continuous stretch of land.

Patrilocality (residence of a married couple with or near the groom's parents) is the nominal rule, although it is followed only about seventy percent of the time. In practice, a man may build his house anywhere, given sufficient incentive (options on the land of his wife's family or a relative's family, or strife within his own family). A specific site is sometimes chosen by taking a handful of soil from each potential site to any person with prophetic powers, who informs the inquirer which site will bring health and prosperity. Some patrilocal joint families existed during the nineteenth century, coming into existence to reduce payments of the "smoke tax" (*yatis geber*), a tax levied by the Amhara feudal elite upon the owner of each home. A joint family usually consisted of a man, his wife, their unmarried children, and their married sons with their families. Such families had partitioned quarters (*sabitara*) in one large house so that each family had its own area for sleeping, preparing food, and storage. At present, newlywed couples usually reside with the husband's parents for a few years, after which they erect a house of their own adjoining the house of the husband's father. This practice has been observed by Nagash and his wife Almaz, who is twenty-seven years of age, and by Bitaw and his wife Sahay, who is eighteen years of age.

Construction of houses and other domestic structures starts during the dry season after the harvest and sometimes continues into the rainy season. The work is usually done by the patrilocal extended family. The planning, and most of the manual labor, is thus done by Erada and his sons. They prepare the materials first and then bring them to the construction site. Beams, rafters, and center poles are hewn or cut from newly felled trees by the sons. Branches of trees are collected and are cut to desired lengths for wattles as the work progresses. The wives haul water for making the mixture of mud and manure, which is prepared by the men and daubed on the wattles by women. Should persons who are not members of the extended family be working, food and drink will be specially served once or twice a day in conjunction with the construction. According to a custom, not followed by all, Erada sacrifices a chicken and holds a minor feast to bless a new house. This rite includes pouring the sacred beverage *meski*, a variety of beer, on the ground in front of the dwelling.

The Sacred Sites

Sacred sites are a vital and integral part of each Qemant community. The relatively great number of these sites and their importance to the average Qemant are among the factors which markedly differentiate Qemant communities from those of neighboring peoples. The Qemant have always preferred to worship in the open, and their most important site of worship is the *degena*,[1] a sacred grove of trees which may cover several acres. Sacred groves are named after and dedicated to culture heroes and are of two distinct types, ceremonial and burial. A ceremonial grove is used for worship only once a year, on a fixed holiday. However, the Qemant constantly show respect for the groves in their day-to-day affairs. For example, if a person has to swear an oath to complete a certain action, he will go to a sacred grove to make the oath. Each community has its own degena. Karkar, with seven groves, has the largest number. Despite the tradition of open-air worship, the *wambar* of Chelga, who is the chief Qemant religious and political leader, uses a prayer house (*shawang*) for many religious activities. This prayer house was built because the Qemant did not wish to conduct religious ceremonies openly in an increasingly Christian religious environment.

---

[1] The word *degena* is used frequently in this work and will not be italicized hereafter. Other Ethiopian words used frequently will be italicized only when first introduced or defined.

A portion of Karkar Anchaw Mikael, from the lofty abode of the Aymba Qole *which overlooks this topographically rugged community. On the horizon between the two center hills is lake Tana. The area in the photograph is* wayna dega.

Sites where major spirits, genii loci called *qole,* are worshipped are second in importance as places of worship. The qole site is smaller than the sacred grove, and is used for venerating a local spirit who can be reached only at his particular abode. Sites of qole worship are in high places, almost always on hilltops or on the edge of an escarpment. They are usually marked by a single tall tree or a prominent rock or pinnacle.

A few sites similar to those used in veneration of qole are used to honor the Qemant God, Adara/Mezgana, and other members of the Qemant pantheon. The most important such site is Adari Fardada (Adara's horse), located near Jalshev in Chelga. The site is marked by a lone, prominent tree on a hilltop where the hoofprints of the horse of God are said to be found in the stones. At some time in the remote past, God, astride his horse, touched the earth on this hill in order to visit humans.

Still other sacred areas, at which no ceremonies are conducted, are burial places of past wambars. The bodies of the last three wambars of Karkar are buried in a hallowed spot on an escarpment called Aberakerna. On a flat-topped hill in Karkar, at Kematayna (Qemant assembly place), a gigantic wild fig tree grows out of the grave of the wambar Jargi. The tree was planted over his grave some three-hundred years ago when this Qemant leader was buried. A peasant can clearly see the wambar's power over fertility when he beholds this unusually large growth. Seven other former wambars of Karkar are buried on this hill. Within the last few years a Christian church called Karkar Madahane Alam (Medicine, or Savior, of the World) was built at Kematayna, and is an example of the centuries-old Ethiopian practice of grafting a Christian church or shrine onto an Agaw religious site.

Other sites of religious significance are stone cairns used as wayside shrines that are on trails near the sacred groves. They have no specific names, and no supernatural being is directly associated with them. Some of the more prominent shrines have an elongated vertical stone implanted in the midst of the cairn, and stained black from many years of anointment with butter. Whether pagan or Christian, Qemant who travel on these trails will sit on a stone slab by the cairn and pray to the culture hero for whom the nearby grove is named. A typical prayer runs: "Thank you, Lord, for You had me reach this place safely. Allow me to be successful in what I am about to do." An offering of a bit of whatever produce the traveler is carrying is then left in front of the cairn.

4

The Pagan-Hebraic Religion

Q EMANT SAY that they have only one God, but their religion includes belief in other supernatural beings and we can say that it constitutes a pantheon. The pantheon consists of a Sky God, holy culture heroes, other holy beings, and genii loci. There is also a concept of a demon. Ceremonies center on a sacrificial offering of blood made by the priests on behalf of the populace to the members of the pantheon.

Religion and the Qemant

The pagan-Hebraic religion of the Qemant is the focal point of this closely knit ethnic group, providing its members with a sense of group identity, reinforcing their basic values, and rigidly defining the social boundaries between them and their neighbors. When a non-Qemant of Ethiopia is asked what the Qemant are like, the answer is in terms of religion, pointing out that religion makes the Qemant distinctive from other Ethiopian peoples. It makes sense, then, to begin investigation of Qemant culture with religion, rather than with some other important aspect of culture such as social organization or economics. Religion is considered here as consisting of all supernaturalism in Qemant culture—not just of beliefs concerning animistic (spiritual) beings.

The religion of the Qemant may be viewed as a pattern of behavior that screens their society from outside cultural influences. Qemant keep their religious beliefs and practices secret, as noted by European travelers in Abyssinia and often mentioned by members of neighboring ethnic groups. Knowledge of the religion is limited to the strictly defined Qemant ethnic group; thus a "closed" system is maintained against the outside world. The *wambars* (arch-politicoreligious leaders of the Qemant), higher and lower priests, and persons holding lesser positions give Qemant culture its distinctive character for they preserve the pagan-Hebraic religion of this archaic sociocultural system.

Religion has helped the Qemant to survive as a distinct ethnic group despite centuries of acculturative pressure from the surrounding Amhara. Many Qemant were compelled, however, to adopt Christianity during the 1880s, under a program of enforced Amharization carried out by Emperor Johannes IV, and this broke down the boundary-maintaining mechanisms supplied by the Qemant religion and spurred the eventual atrophy of Qemant society and culture.

Culture is often considered to be a complex of extrasomatic adaptations to environment. Qemant religion may be viewed as a fundamental cultural adaptation of this kind. Religion may, indeed, be as important an adaptation as is technology. Because the preindustrial technology of the Qemant peasantry cannot control the environment with any degree of certainty and cannot provide techniques for explaining natural phenomena, Qemant must resort to supernaturalism in their attempts to control and to explain.

A Qemant need not feel impotent when faced with vicissitudes of nature or feel overwhelmed when confronted by a seemingly inexplicable event. He uses religion to manipulate the environment for a needed or desired end. It is not important that the supernatural cause often has no real effect. Most ill people get well, crops invariably mature, livestock usually prospers, and, in general, one tends to recollect good experiences rather than misfortunes. Religious faith can also heal and blight men, for we are psychosomatic beings and not just organisms. The main point is that religion provides a sense of well-being and security, allowing tension-reducing activity to be directed against threats so that the individual and society can continue to function without the psychic or social disorganization that eminates from doubt and fear. Similarly, assigning a supernatural cause to a seemingly unfathomable phenomenon allows the otherwise unknown to become known. Motivations of anthropomorphic spirits or human religious practitioners thought to control the supernatural "causes" answer the "why" just as the concept of supernatural cause answers the "how" of an occurrence.

The Qemant live in a supernatural as well as natural universe, and they can generally distinguish between these two universes—in other words, distinguish the sacred from the profane. However, they cannot always specifically do so because they lack sufficient empirical data in each given instance, since their technology is inadequate for the gathering of such information.

The Religion of the Ancestral Agaw Peoples

From historical evidence and ethnographic survivals we can reconstruct a broad outline of the religion of the ancestral Agaw before southern Arabic and Hebraic religious elements arrived. The religion of the primitive Agaw horticulturalists probably included a Sky God, regarded as a very remote being; genii loci; personal spirits; and sky spirits, minor deities who were sometimes culture heroes. Certain individual trees and some animals, such as serpents, were also worshipped. Groves of trees, single trees, hilltops, and streams were places of religious ceremonies and were often thought to be abodes of supernatural beings.

Evidence indicates that the Agaw had no formally organized priesthood in earliest times; instead, shamans served as mediums through whom the spirits of the supernatural world contacted the Agaw. Eventually, a priesthood arose with duties that included interceding with a pantheon on behalf of the people, insuring fertility of the fields and, at times, regulating rain. The priests were sometimes political administrators as well. The shamans were not replaced by the priests, but were relegated to roles of lesser prestige as informal religious practitioners and exist as such today.

At later dates, elements of other religions diffused to the Agaw and syncretism resulted. Many elements of the ancestral pagan-Agaw religion survived. Since the Qemant adopted fewer Hebraic and Christian elements in their religion than any other Agaw group, their religion retains the largest pagan substratum to be found in the northern and central parts of the Ethiopian high plateau.

Off To Visit the Wambar of Chelga

Early in my fieldwork experience, when the rivers had subsided, I set out to visit the last Qemant wambar, the chief politicoreligious leader of the group. This was a necessary first step in my study of the Qemant and their religion. The auto journey over a rough motor track to the village of Aykel in Chelga took over 6 hours since my assistant, Alemayehu Gesese, and I had to chop down a sapling growing in the track, level innumerable ruts and gullies, and raise many fords in stream beds by filling them with rocks. Further, we had to break up and remove outcroppings of rock when they protruded into our path. By the time we reached Aykel, I felt like a convict on a road gang. Needless to say, the people of Aykel were fascinated with my Volkswagen and found it difficult to believe that such a small vehicle had traveled so far into the hinterland. I was rather surprised myself!

After sending word to the wambar that we would like an audience with him, we pitched our tent and made camp. Two days later the religious leader sent a guide who led us from Aykel over a path toward the wambar's homestead. As we walked, our guide pointed out an immense sacred grove of trees and the place where the hooves of God's horse had imprinted the ground. After walking a short distance, we were greeted by a younger brother of the wambar, who conducted us into Jalshev, the wambar's large homestead. The homestead, comprised of many houses, was encircled with eucalypti, some native trees, and a knee-high stone wall.

The wambar had made contact with only a few Westerners and Western cultural elements and had never, of course, seen a Hollywood motion picture, but his theatrical preparations for my visit in no way disappointed my expectations. My assistant and I were solemnly ushered into a "meeting" house of round plan on the edge of the homestead. Inside, about two-thirds of the otherwise bare, earthen walls were covered by white cloth mounted on poles, and green boughs of fragrant eucalyptus were strewn upon the earthen floor. A mud bench covered with a reddish rug was built into the remaining third of the wall. Flanked by two priests, the wambar sat upon this platform; his mother sat at his feet. Wambar Maluna Mersha, clothed in white with a white turban and a dark blue cape embroidered in gold, was a tall, rather stocky man. (His stature may be due to the better-than-average diet his priestly lineage has enjoyed through the centuries.) As we entered, we gave the wambar a deep bow, but did not kiss his knees or feet as others normally do, for this procedure would have ritually contaminated him.

After seating ourselves in the chairs offered, we stated the purpose of our visit and I gave the religious leaders a brief overview of my fieldwork, including what I knew of Qemant society and its history. My interest in their way of life made a favorable impression on all present, including many laymen, but the wambar was very reserved and gave us only a well-hedged approval for the fieldwork. After much negotiating that day and the next, we received permission to visit his homestead from time to time, to pitch our tent next to his house, and to attend all ceremonies. As the months passed and we took part in rites in the prescribed manner, scrupulously observed all taboos, and gave warm positive comments to all that we observed and participated in, the religious leaders and elders became more friendly, some extremely so. However, the wambar was always to remain somewhat aloof and enigmatic.

Following our conversations of the first morning meeting, *selah* and *miz* (native beer and a honey-water, respectively) were served to all present, and the priests led the Qemant in prayer. This, and all discussion concerning us between the wambar and his priests, was conducted in Qemantinya. We were then fed, but no one else ate because all feared ritual pollution from eating with non-Qemant. By the time the spring fertility rites were conducted, we were eating with the Qemant leaders, but only from a separate basket.

Off to visit the wambar of Chelga. Scene is a mile north of Jalshev during dry season.

As I moved socially closer to the wambar and other religious figures, my knowledge of the Qemant religion, so basic to their very existence, increased. However, I constantly checked the accuracy of their information against my own observations and against information gathered from Qemant laymen and non-Qemant.

World View and Basic Values

As with other ethnic groups, the religion of the Qemant depicts in large measure their world view. A world view is not only rather explicit in aspects of culture such as religion, mythology, and folklore; it is partly tacit in, and might be inferred from, the ethnological study of the structure of the culture containing the world view. One element of Qemant world outlook stresses the group's uniqueness and makes mandatory social separation from other peoples. Furthermore, just as their society has a dual organization, Qemant believe the universe is dually organized into realms of good and evil. Adherence to pagan-Hebraic behavioral rules means eternal existence in a paradise of the good.

Religions of some ethnic groups are related, in varying degrees, to the preservation of the society's basic values or central behavioral rules. The Qemant are most certainly among the societies whose religious beliefs are closely integrated with their code of ethics. A religion like that of the Qemant, which provides ultimate, and usually supernatural, sanctions for a society's rules of behavior, fulfills vital, society-preserving functions. One such function serves to defend the group against alien behavior from outside and against deviant behavior from within. Another integrates the group through ritual reinforcement of mores and reacknowledgment of the sacredness of the group, upon which the existence of the individual is dependent. Reinforcement and reacknowledgment occur each time a Qemant attends one of many societally cohesive rites. These rites are noted at appropriate points in this book.

Qemant outlook on the universe retains some old, deep-rooted beliefs about God and the soul which are generally Hebraic. However, the ultimate origin of some of the beliefs may not be Hebraic, as in the case of the cold and fiery hell and its opposition to heaven, mentioned below. Qemant believe that the soul (fiwa) resides in every part of the body. Upon death, the soul leaves the body and goes to samayi, a point in the sky from which one's soul is dispatched to heaven (ganat) or hell (siol), according to one's behavior while alive. The original Qemant belief may have been that one's soul went into the sky, samayi, to reside with God. According to the wambar, "In heaven, people perform no labor, live in fine houses, and have much honey," but "Hell has no food; there is fire everywhere; and it is very cold."

In order for the soul to reach heaven, wambars teach that a Qemant should observe the following laws (to which I have assigned numbers as a matter of convenience): (1) Do not steal. (2) Do not copulate with or take the wife of another man. (3) Do not perform other evil deeds. (4) If a person has wronged you, do not avenge yourself; relegate vengeance to God. (5) One woman should have one husband and one man should have one wife. (6) If you see someone doing wrong, do not inform the feudal officials. The first four rules are related to minimizing strife and disunity in Qemant society, and seem to be ancient. The fifth rule has a probable origin in recent Christian doctrine, as it opposes older Qemant practice, as noted in the oral history and mythology. The sixth rule, if observed, would help maintain Qemant societal boundaries in opposition to the enveloping Amhara feudal structure.

During my stay among the Qemant, they gradually began to confide in me that they believe God will come to earth upon his horse for the Last Judgment (*shamhula*) of the good and evil ones. Thus "good" Qemant will be given the ultimate reward for their behavior, customs sustaining Qemant society. The date of the Last Judgment is unknown; it might be any Sabbath (dusk on Friday until dusk on Saturday) and Qemant, like Erada and his family, must always be ready for this eventuality.

Until very recently, Qemant in the Karkar area thought the Sabbath of the Last Judgment might be on the same weekend as their ceremony for Entala, a culture heroine. The holiday of Entala is also the same day as the Christian holiday called *Dabra Zayt* (Mount of Olives, but, in more accurate translation into English, Passion Sunday). On Friday night the Qemant, as a group, prepared for the Last Judgment by praying, washing the body, and wearing fresh clothing. At present, the practice is continued by many Christian Qemant who say it is in honor of Christ on the Mount of Olives. The practice of the Qemant in Chelga of holding their annual fertility ceremony on what is now Passion Sunday is another indication of the pre-Christian importance of the day.

The Qemant Pantheon

Qemant priests claim that their religion is monotheistic because they have "one God." However, this God is but one of many supernatural beings, some of whom can be considered minor deities. Thus we shall speak of a Qemant pantheon even though one of the deities is now considered most supreme. This consideration originates in Hebraic influence on Qemant religion.

MEZGANA, THE SKY GOD. According to Qemant, their God is male and resides in the sky. He is not different in reality from the ancient Agaw Sky God and somewhat resembles the Hebrew God worshipped by the Hebrao-pagan Falasha Agaw. Belief in the ancient Sky God is one of the principal traits that distinguishes the Qemant from their neighbors, who abhor such a marked manifestation of paganism. At this point we should state that data from fieldwork indicate that the Qemant do not worship the sun, as mentioned by some European scholars. The Qemant face east during prayer because they believe it is the direction of Jerusalem and not because it is the direction of the rising sun.

The term used by the Qemant to identify the Sky God is *Adara,* and they sometimes prefix the term with "my" (*ye*). The Falasha of Qwara, who still speak Agaw, use the same word for "God." The Qemant Adara is named *Mezgana,* and the Falasha Adara has at least two names, *Elohe* and *Adonay.* Qemant believe

Mezgana is omnipresent, omnipotent, and omniscient, and that everything was created by Him; therefore, He has the right to destroy everything. He is an anthropomorphic God; Qemant say, "Mezgana looks like man."

Although members of the Qemant priesthood sometimes contact Mezgana directly, they usually reach Him through intermediary culture heroes called *qedus*. *Qedus* means "saint" and "holy" and applies to the spirits of dead human beings who are culture heroes and to angelic beings. Some of the beings in these two categories originally may have been minor deities.

CULTURE HEROES. In Qemantland, every culture hero has his own sacred grove. Once each year, at times varying according to the holiday of the particular culture hero, a major ceremony is held in each grove during which the mythological hero is venerated. Mezgana is also said to be worshipped at this time. The culture hero is a "holy intermediary" and is expected to intercede with Mezgana on behalf of the Qemant assembled that day. The practice of the Agaw, Amhara, and Tegre is to have some powerful supernatural being intercede in making an appeal to God. (It is interesting to note that in the secular life of these societies, appeals for aid to people holding positions of authority are also made through intermediaries.) Holy culture heroes of the Qemant are, for the most part, the ancestral heads of the clans in the Keber moiety, the more important of the two Qemant moieties. Other culture heroes include ancestors of these heads and certain wives of the ancestors.

Because the culture heroes of the clans are ever present in their groves, they provide another cohesive religious bond for the Qemant, a bond without parallel among their neighbors. The groves are a direct link from this world to Mezgana in heaven. Qemant believe that holy men, when alone in a sacred grove, can pray so intensely to Mezgana that these men will contact Him and then disappear from the earth. Various myths attest to such events. Culture heroes' groves are more than sites where heaven impinges upon the earth; they remind the average Qemant that Mezgana is very much alive and that His religion should be fervently embraced.

Myths are sacred tales explaining, often justifying and supporting, a cultural element and sometimes explaining natural phenomena. Qemant mythology functions to link the people with the past and their culture heroic ancestors who first settled Qemantland, thus validating present-day claims to land. For example, the wambar of Chelga counts back through fourteen remembered generations (many have undoubtedly been lost through the centuries) to the culture hero ancestral to his clan. In addition, these sacred tales reinforce the religious behavior basic to societal preservation.

Qemant mythology begins with Yaner, also called Aynar, who appears to be the oldest culture hero. Little is known about him, and many people replace him in legends with his son, Aydarki. Yaner is called by some "the first Qemant in Ethiopia," as are his son and grandson, Aydarki and Keberwa. Because they want their religion to appear less pagan and more Hebraic, some Qemant recount an Hebraized genealogy of the culture heroes. Thus, a few informants said that Yaner is the grandson of Canaan, the fourth son of Ham, son of Noah. According to some legends, Canaan's son, Arwadi, came to Ethiopia from the land of

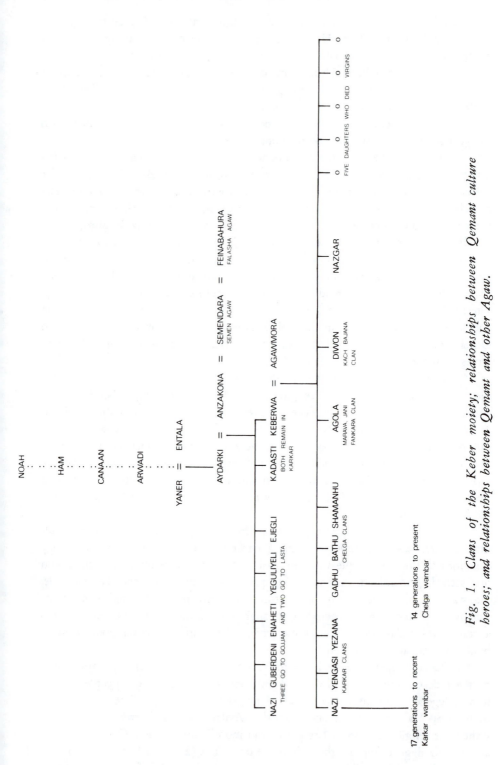

Fig. 1. Clans of the Keber moiety; relationships between Qemant culture heroes; and relationships between Qemant and other Agaw.

Canaan to found the Qemant group, whereas in other legends Arwadi's son, Yaner, did so. (See Fig. 1.) Both accounts might be called examples of ancestral enoblement rather than dim memories of ancestral migration. All agree that Yaner had a wife called Entala.

During a seven-year drought (an allusion to the biblical seven lean years?), Aydarki, the son of Yaner and Entala, told everyone to assemble on a mountaintop to pray to Mezgana for rain. Before the people returned home, rain fell. Within three months, seeds sown seven years earlier had grown and ripened. Qemant priests today pray in similar fashion to ask for rain. The Qemant, by recounting the myth of the seven-year drought, are reminded of the efficacy of this religious observance, one of many permeating the lives of every Qemant. Aydarki's wife, Anzakona, is sometimes identified with the Virgin Mary, a syncretization of the nineteenth century.

Mythology gives the Qemant an historical schema from which they can determine their place among other peoples. For example, the idea that all Agaw groups are ethnically related is expressed in myths about the sons of Aydarki, who are regarded as the ancestors of the various groups of Agaw. Aydarki and Anzakona had seven sons, of whom three went to the Agaw area called Lasta, two went to the Agaw area in Gojjam, and two went to what is now Karkar. Some Qemant say Aydarki has two other wives, reflecting earlier Agaw customs of polygyny. The first of these wives is Semendara, the mother of the Agaw of Semen, and the second is Feinabahura (Falasha child), the mother of the Falasha.

Kadasti and Keberwa are the sons of Aydarki and Anzakona who settled in what is now Karkar. Kadasti had no children. His groves are in Karkar, Chanchuq, and Gava-Galagar. Keberwa is the most important culture hero of the Qemant, and his name, Keber, is given to the patrimoiety with the greater prestige. Qemant say Keberwa lived in the vicinity of a grove named for him just beyond the southern border of Karkar. The wambar of Chelga always received in this grove the ceremony of validation of office, conducted by the Karkar wambar. Keberwa had nine sons, who are worshipped as saints (*qedus*). Two sons, Gadhu and Bathu, are said to have acquired the Qemant lands from a king of the Falasha Agaw who gave them as much land as they could ride across on horseback before sunset. Gadhu stopped the sun for three days to increase the amount of land that could be acquired in this way. This tale helps validate Qemant claims to land and reflects animosity between the Qemant and the once formidable Falasha.

ANGELS. In addition to its meaning of culture hero, the term *qedus* is also applied to other supernatural beings that are now equated with Hebrao-Christian angels. Originally, these beings were probably sky spirits or minor deities. A qedus named Jakaranti is identified as the angel St. Michael. Gergeliwali and Gebarhu are called angels, but have no Hebrao-Christian equivalents. Gabrael is probably an addition from Hebrao-Christian beliefs (the angel Gabriel) because he has no other native Qemant name. It is likely, in fact, that the concept of angels among the Qemant is Hebraic, stemming from the period when all groups of the Agaw received elements of the Hebrew religion.

OTHER HOLY FIGURES. The Qemant religion also acquired some Hebraic biblical figures. For example, one frequently hears the name Abraham used in blessings: "Let your house be as Abraham's house, and let God make you as prosperous as Abraham was." Adam is "the first person created by Mezgana, and the source of all people." Moses (Muse) is alluded to when the Qemant chant "*tabota* Muse" (ark of the covenant of Moses), which is used in many ceremonies. Nevertheless, Moses is not very important in the only partially Hebraized mythology of the Qemant. Legend tells that Aydarki asked Moses to be his witness in a dispute, but Moses hid the truth and thus gave false witness. Because Aydarki was very angry, Moses "vanished." Today, when a person holds back some information, the others will say, "It is Moses," meaning the person is hiding the truth as Moses did. The Scottish traveler James Bruce said the Qemant avoid eating fish because they believe they are descendants of Jonah (Yonas). This is a just-so story; a taboo against eating fish is found among all speakers of Cushitic languages, and the Qemant have no knowledge of Jonah.

GENII LOCI. Beside the natural and visible human and animal life in Qemantland, there are supernatural beings only indirectly apparent. The most important of these are genii loci, spirits always present at their abodes. They are minor deities who have strong control over limited areas, usually part or the whole of a single community. A genius loci is called a qole and is referred to by the name of the place where it is venerated, for example, the Gejan Qole and the Aymba Qole. The word qole is also used to mean personal guardian spirits, which we shall discuss later. Worship of genii loci is ancient in the religion of the Qemant and the Kumfal Agaw. The Awiya and Falasha Agaw also worship these spirits, but to a lesser extent. Many Christian Amhara, including priests, also venerate genii loci, although this practice is not officially permitted or recognized by the Church.

Community tensions caused by locusts, strife, disease, or the need to regulate rain can be eased by proper veneration of the genii loci. The Aymba Qole in Karkar, whose abode is an area on a hilltop where there is a single, large tree, is regularly worshipped in order to increase rainfall at the beginning of the agricultural season. The Gejan Qole is venerated a few miles to the west at a rocky pinnacle on the edge of the escarpment which bisects Karkar. This spirit is requested to reduce or end rainfall toward the end of the agricultural season. The entire community participates in ceremonies honoring qoles, which feature sacrificial offerings by animal blood. White bulls or white sheep contributed by community members are slaughtered for this purpose by Qemant priests. Ordinarily, only one animal is sacrificed. The qole is said to "drink" the blood as it soaks into the ground. The priests eat part of the flesh of the animal, cooked or raw, and bury the remainder at the qole's abode. This abode is occasionally a sacred grove not connected with a culture hero.

Before Hebraic religious elements were syncretized with the pagan religion of the Qemant, qoles and the sky spirits were more important in the daily religious routine of the Qemant than Mezgana, who was then remote from daily life. Although below Mezgana in the modern pantheon, these supernatural beings are still very important and are worshipped regularly.

Saytan

Saytan, a name that is derived from the Satan of Hebraic belief, is a supernatural being known to most Agaw groups. He is also known by the Ethiopian name of Ganel, and Saytan-Ganel appears to be another example of the merging of Agaw and Hebraic beliefs. Saytan is the essence of all that is evil. Qemant, Amhara, and Falasha uniformly conceive of Saytan as being very black and horrible-looking, having human or animal form, and possessing great powers, including the ability to cause thunder and lightning.

A person may acquire evil powers by entering into a league with Saytan. Such a person is called Ganel *sabi* (Ganel puller). One can also become a Ganel sabi by defecating and urinating at the outer of the three concentric walls of a circular Ethiopian church. As in the tale of Dr. Faustus, the Ganel sabi must pay for his evil powers with his immortal soul. A Ganel sabi can kill people, burn houses from a distance, cure people with Saytan's advice, and cause other fortune or misfortune. The services of a Ganel sabi may be purchased for goods or money. Many people believe that Saytan and his Ganel sabis are found on mountaintops and in rivers, as are qoles. This belief suggests a syncretism of Hebrew beliefs of Satan and Agaw beliefs about qole, some of whom are regarded as malevolent.

Saytan's power is often invoked by reading certain passages from a book. Since few other people in Ethiopia are literate, Christian, Muslim, and Falasha priests are all called Ganel sabis at times. Until very recently, most books in Ethiopia were religious, written for Christians and Falasha in the ancient Ethiopic or Geez, and for Muslims in classical Arabic. These hand-copied manuscripts are sacred and are held in awe by the illiterate peasantry, which cannot share the power imparted to the literate by their ability to gain the knowledge contained in them. Here we note that writing is a weapon used by the feudal and religious elite against the peasants.

The Priesthood ·

WAMBARS. The wambar is the chief religious and political leader of the Qemant, and his position greatly distinguishes the Qemant from other groups in northern and central Ethiopia, whose leaders do not hold such dual positions of leadership. Political aspects of roles of the wambars and other members of the priesthood are treated in Chapter 6. Priests, it may be added, are organized into a hierarchy and must learn formalized ritual patterns in order to act as middlemen for communication between humans and the beings of their animistic world.

The wambar personifies what is distinctively "Qemant," as he is a paragon of propriety and is the supreme earthly guardian of the behavior of members of the society. He officiates at major ceremonies where priests perform rituals attempting to manipulate nature through supplication of members of the pantheon. The wambar makes life secure for the Qemant by praying to regulate the weather, to end disease or other personal misfortune, to eradicate dangerous wild animals, and to punish transgressors of laws. His most important act is praying for the dead during the rite of passage which follows funerals, to assure their entry into heaven.

The wambar also insures fertility in people and in nature. A barren woman gives him an offering in return for prayers. The highlight of the annual ceremonial calendar is the spring fertility rite performed by the wambar. The wambar makes no sacrifices; indeed, he cannot hold a knife or any weapon in his hand, and his food must be cut for him.

Two positions as superior wambars exist, one in Karkar, which has been unfilled since the mid-1950s, and one in Chelga. Some other communities formerly had wambars who held positions subordinate to the wambars at Chelga and Karkar. These lesser wambars did not survive a phase of forced Amharization of the 1880s.

Wambar Mulunah Marsha, the chief political and religious leader of the Qemant.

When a wambar is old or dies, the Qemant males elect a successor from the Keber moiety, which has greater prestige than the Yetanti moiety. The wambar of Chelga is chosen by election from members of certain priestly lineages of the Bathu, Gadhu, and Shamanhu clans, and the wambar of Karkar is similarly chosen from priestly lineages of the Nazi, Engesi, and Yezana clans.

The last wambar elected in Karkar, whose name was Asrasa, assumed office at the age of fifty-six in the reign of Menelek II (1889–1913). Wambar Asrasa was from the Nazi patriclan. He was succeeded by wambar Gosha of the Yengasi patriclan, who held the position for five years. Sometime around 1915 Asrasa's son, Gonet, became wambar at forty-six years of age—by agreement among the people rather than by election. At that time, about one-half of the Qemant in Karkar had become Christians. The position of wambar was fraught with tension and turmoil and did not have all of its former remuneration; thus, not many men in the three clans in Karkar wanted the position. Wambar Gonet, previously a *kamazana,* or higher priest, died in Gondar shortly before 1955 without a successor.

The names and other information are available on the last eight wambars of Chelga. The two earliest, Begaba and Aykel, bore Qemantinya names; the more recent ones had Amharic names. (Personal genealogies that were collected indicate the Qemant shifted to Amharic names four or five generations ago, sometime between 1800 and 1850. This is an example of Qemant adaptation of an Amhara culture trait before the enforced phase of Amharization.)

A Chelga wambar was elected in 1889 and his successor in 1929. When the latter died in 1941, the present wambar, Mulunah Marsha, was elected. Since he was only six years old when elected, his father officiated for him until he came of age. At present, wambar Mulunah Marsha has about five-hundred followers who have not been baptized as Christians.

After being selected, a wambar-elect is blessed by the people and, when selection is not a replacement caused by death, by the wambar whom he is succeeding. He is showered with green grass and leaves, an allusion to his powers over fertility. Then, the people say, "Let the land be blessed by you; let it be peaceful, respected, prosperous, and healthy." The wambar-elect is then educated by the wambar and the older priests. Before he can assume office, the wambar-elect must ordinarily complete his education and the old wambar must have died. At the time he takes office, the wambar-elect goes to a grove for a ceremonial blessing of his white turban. This ceremony is followed on the same day by two other ceremonies, the *yaqumtazkar,* given by a person for himself so that he may go to heaven, and the *kasa,* a rite of passage administered by priests, which the wambar and other priests undergo when they are ordained. Following these rites, a wambar has power over priests and laymen. The wambar of Chelga then makes a trip to Karkar with gifts for the wambar of Karkar, who holds in Keberwa grove a ceremony of validation and blessing for him. Following the ceremony, a two- or three-day visit begins, with the wambar of Karkar providing food and drink for his guests from Chelga. Tradition has it that in the nineteenth century and earlier the wambar of Chelga would make an annual visit with gifts to his superior in Karkar.

The kamazana, *or higher priest, of the community of Chelga dressed in a white toga and turban with a horse-tail fly whisk in hand.*

Qemant must work three days each year for the wambar of their region; one day each is given to plowing, weeding, and harvesting. In recent decades, since the end of the payment of taxes by Qemant to the wambar, this mandatory labor has been a major source of the wambar's wealth. Qemant pay the wambar with bars of salt for various ministrations, and grain and livestock are given to him for use in the major ceremonies. In addition, he is often given the choice, upper portion of the hind limbs of sheep and cattle slaughtered for feasts.

HIGHER AND LOWER PRIESTS. Under the wambar are two levels of priests. The higher, called *kamazana,* is elected from the Keber moiety, and the lower, *abayegariya,* is elected from the Yetanti moiety. Like the wambar, the priests must come from certain lineages in certain clans that have traditionally supplied the personnel for these religious positions. After a man has been elected to priesthood by the community, he is taken by the people to the wambar, who blesses him and confirms his appointment. For these services, the wambar receives two bars of salt or two Maria Theresas (silver "dollars"). The priest then begins training for his new role. Observing and participating in ceremonies are important parts of the training. After a few years of instruction, the priest goes before the wambar, who presents him with a white turban which has been blessed. Then, like the wambar, the priest receives the rites of kasa and yaqumtazkar, which constitute the final events of ordainment. The wambar can control the behavior of a priest by levying fines for infractions of priestly duties or conduct. Such fines range from a bar of salt to a cow, according to the nature of the misconduct.

Each community has at least one higher priest and one lower priest, who work together in all ceremonies. During ceremonies of sacrifice, the higher priest cuts with a knife the throat of the ox, sheep, goat, or chicken while the lower priest holds the animal's legs. Each priest has certain roles, chanting and singing together and separately. The lower priest plays a lyre (*bagana*) in the ceremonies. Both pray to regulate weather and to cure animals. When livestock is diseased, the priests gather all the animals about them and pray. One of the priests at this time holds in his arms a sheep, which is carried around the animals. The sheep is then killed and its blood is sprinkled over the other animals.

Priests are remunerated with bars of salt for their services in performing the ritual in various rites of passage, rain-regulating ceremonies, and curing ceremonies such as the one with the livestock. The major source of priestly income, however, comes from labor which adult males in each community must supply to the local priests. Like the wambar, each priest receives three days of agricultural labor: one each of plowing, weeding, and harvesting. Priests also receive food in the form of meals whenever members of the community hold feasts, to which the priests are always invited.

MINOR POLITICORELIGIOUS POSITIONS. Three positions that entail both religious and political duties are not included in the priesthood. The most important of these is the spokesman (*afaliq*), who is chosen by the wambar from the Keber moiety. The spokesman's duties are to conduct investigations for the wambar and to attempt to settle disputes. The subjects of the investigations are disagreements among the peasants and infractions of pagan-Hebraic law. The second position is as majordomo (*galasim*) at ceremonies. Selected from the Keber moiety, the majordomo oversees the serving of the ordinary beer and the special bread made of chick peas (*shemkura*) that are consumed during ceremonies. If there is not enough food, he can order the people to bring more. The third position is as *mashana*. Selected from the Yetanti moiety, the *mashana* carries the sacred beer (*meski*) to the ceremonies, serving and watching over it.

5

Spirits and Practitioners outside the Qemant Pantheon and Priesthood

THE PERSONAL SPIRITS, personal qoles, jinn, and specific spirits of disease discussed below are acknowledged and venerated by Qemant, by other Agaw, and by Christian and Muslim Amhara. A legend concerning the origin of these spirits is common to the Qemant and their neighbors. Adam and Eve had many children. One day God asked Eve to show Him all of the children, but she brought Him only thirty and hid the others. God said, "Let the ones that you hid be hidden forever, and let the ones that you showed be forever visible." Another version describes fifteen fair and fifteen ugly children. Eve hid the fair ones, whom "God curses to live in darkness and shadows." The "visible" childern are the progenitors of living people and the "hidden" ones of spirits who live in shade, in water, and with people as personal spirits. Many of the spirits are said to protect people and to pray to God on their behalf.

Zar, A Personal Spirit

SHAMANISM. Ayo, who is Erada's brother and fifty-four years of age, is like most Qemant a plowman, but he also serves as a part-time religious practitioner. Ayo deals with zars and other personal spirits, performing the role of *balazar* (master of the zar), usually in a special house of his homestead about 1000 feet from that of Erada. Balazars may also belong to other groups of Agaw or may be Christian or Muslim Amhara, but they never become priests in any religion. In anthropological classification, the balazar is a shaman, one who acquires his supernatural power and his social position from his ability to contact directly animistic (spiritual) beings. These are usually minor spirits for whom the shaman serves as a medium or "mouthpiece" when the spirit takes possession of him. Shamans of the Qemant and neighboring peoples are additionally often leaders of cults addressed to personal spirits.

Shamanism is usually found in technologically primitive, simply organized hunting and gathering and horticultural societies. Priesthoods, however, usually occur in technologically advanced and more socially complex horticultural and agricultural societies. In Qemantland, balazars like Ayo and the zar-like spirits are survivals of the time when the primitive Agaw had not yet developed a formal priesthood and pantheon. In this early period, the Agaw religion had an aloof Sky God, and the ceremonial focus was on the shamans and lesser spirits. Such a shamanistic religious organization was found among the technologically primitive Kumfal Agaw until only a few years ago. No evidence supports the idea suggested by some scholars that the zar was once the Agaw Sky God whose status later declined to that of a personal spirit.

ZAR. The zars are the most important of the personal spirits of the Qemant and neighboring peoples. Any person may have a zar as well as other personal spirits, although most people do not have a zar, and those who do sometimes find that the spirit might not be present for months or years. Zars may be either male or female and are often of the same sex as the human beings with whom they are associated. Although usually benevolent or neutral, when "neglected," zars may become malevolent, causing disease or other misfortune. A zar can possess a person, causing uncontrolled motion and speech. Although all Qemant believe in zars, the wambar and his priests do not recognize or permit rites connected with these spirits.

Ayo's zar, as is customary for the personal spirit of a balazar, is more powerful and knowledgeable than the zars of other persons. It has knowledge Ayo needs to influence other people and to make contact with and obtain information from their personal spirits. Ayo became a shaman by inheriting a spirit from a balazar who was a relative. Others may be "upgraded" to the status of a balazar after having an unusually active zar for several years.

Tall and slender, with gray hair partially encircling his otherwise bald head, Ayo is clad in special white clothing for his shamanistic rites. Some balazars are more colorfully clothed in garments of bright blue and red. They wear long strands of beads, place rings on most fingers, grow their hair long, and may have a small bell or two attached to their person. Often a small rod or a fly whisk of horsehair on a stick is carried in the hand. These "hip" figures would blend into the scene on many American college campuses in recent times, and the comparison is still more apt when one considers the pharmacological source of many of the balazars' entranced states.

Peoples who have problems with their personal spirits, who have a new personal spirit which has not yet adjusted itself, who are discontent in some way, or who seek information—whether it pertains to zars or not—come to Ayo's house. Important shamans like Ayo have a servant called *kadami* who serves coffee, tends the fire, and arranges the shaman's ceremonial house, which may not always be distinct from his dwelling. Like other shamans, Ayo specifies the appointment time, usually during the evening or night, for people capable of becoming possessed. However a person is not usually admitted to evening ceremonies until it is certain that he is capable of being possessed by a zar, and thus capable of fully participating in a zar ceremony. Therefore, Ayo first gives him an audience at another time, often during the daylight. At this daylight appointment, Ayo becomes possessed and acts as a medium for his zar, who speaks through his mouth. Ayo may also try to put the client into a hypnotic trance in which the client is also possessed and becomes a medium. Ayo also travels to the house of any infirm client.

In return for his services, people give the shaman gifts, usually coffee, food, *araqe* (distilled alcoholic liquor), and money. If a person does not receive satisfactory results from one shaman, he may go to another. In fact, a few people go from one shaman to another until they die from a persisting ailment. Some clients have been with Ayo for years, while others try his services for a short time and then select another balazar. Recently, several of Ayo's clients have transferred to a female shaman in a neighboring community.

The shamanistic ceremony begins in the evening and continues throughout the night. In his balazar house, Ayo, seated on a chair or stool, is separated from the assembly by a curtain. The people assembled usually have been initiated previously into Ayo's congregation. To eliminate pretenders who are not capable of an entranced possession, Ayo has a novice beaten, pricked with a sharp object, or rolled into the fire in the central hearth. If the person does not notice the pain, Ayo pronounces him truly possessed by a zar. Following further ritual, the newcomer is admitted to the congregation. Those who are unclean, that is, anyone having had sexual intercourse the previous night or women who are menstruating, may not enter a shaman's house.

WITHIN THE HOUSE OF THE ZAR-MASTER. The screening curtain and the ritual "zar language" employed during the evening ceremonies are part of the facade Ayo uses to create a feeling of awe and mystery in his congregation. The facade constitutes a barrier between himself and any questioning peasant who might want to examine the shamanistic role. Ayo's clients are seated upon the floor, which is strewn with freshly cut grass, in the dark, mud-walled house, their faces illuminated by the flickering fire in the hearth. Ayo is shrouded by the curtain. The walls vibrate with the measured beat of the small, hide-covered ceremonial drum Ayo uses to accompany his shamanistic chant. The participants in the rite join in the chant with their voices and rhythmically clap their hands to the beat of the drum. Some begin to rock to and fro, lost in a deep state of preoccupation.

Pungent fumes from boiling coffee and burning incense displace the air in the crowded house, causing one's head to reel. The abundant visual, auditory, olfactory, and kinesthetic stimuli are supplemented by oral stimuli as the participants drink the distilled liquor *araqe*, and chew *chat*,[1] a mildly narcotic, leafy perennial shrub native to Ethiopia. Aided by these stimulants, various people begin to pulsate and to jerk, entering into a state of possession at intervals during the rite. Such people are called *tashoma* (the appointed or filled one) and "the horse of the zar." They might be possessed by one spirit or by a succession of spirits, but simultaneous possession by more than one spirit is rare.

---

[1] *Catha edulis* is the scientific name of this Ethiopian drug plant containing cathine and celastrine, both alkaloids.

Ayo talks to each person's zar in "the language of the zar" and later interprets these conversations, telling the possessed person how to make his, or her, zar content. While possessed, the participant may speak in his native language and in zar language but the voice, often alien in tone, is said to be that of a zar-spirit speaking through the person's mouth. Zar language varies. The zar of a Muslim shaman may use a few, little-understood phrases from the Koran. Zars of other people may speak in gibberish that is said to be the language of the Galla people of Ethiopia. Some zars use a combination of phrases from alien languages, nonsense syllables, and perfectly pronounced or slurred words from the host's own language. Ventriloquism is sometimes employed by Ayo, whose zar can speak from various parts of the room. A zar may ask the assembled people to sing for him, to bring him a drink, or to perform some other act. If satisfied, the zar may bless the assembled people before he relinquishes control.

Shortly after the beginning of the meeting in the house of the zar-master, one entranced, attractive woman of middle age begins to creep on her hands and knees about the floor, biting and chewing any object within her reach. She bites everyone's clothing and, if they are not careful, some of their limbs. Sitting back on her haunches, the woman opens her mouth and a voice trills, "Give me araqe to drink." After she drinks the strong liquor poured for her zar, the voice of the spirit shrills a thank you and then blesses the people assembled, "Let your foes be like dust, let qole make you prosperous, let the [feudal] officials become your friends, be peaceful and friendly, and be hot-tempered, but not jealous." The woman's zar then asks for water. Ayo orders a basin of water, strewn with grass, to be placed upon the floor near the door. The woman crawls to the basin, picks it up with her teeth, and drinks the water. Finally, she jumps up, a voice screaming and shrieking from within her throat, and begins a frenzied dance lasting five minutes while continuing her assault upon everyone's eardrums. As she whirls and thrashes about, her limbs catch the light of the waning fire. At last she collapses into a quiet and relaxed state and one can again hear the beat of Ayo's drum and the crackling of the fire in the hearth, now refueled by Ayo's silent servant.

A divorced and somewhat older and slighter woman, whose hair is streaked with gray, is the next person to become possessed. At first she sits quietly upon the floor, but suddenly her body becomes contorted and her eyes bulge from her narrow face. A male zar is in possession of her and he says, "Now it is night; there are people to make you happy by beating time with their hands and upon the drum." Then it is silent except for the throb of the drum and the snapping of the fire. Ayo commands the devotees of his zar cult to clap their hands and to chant for the benefit of the woman's zar. A demand for araqe is made by the zar, and the woman consumes almost one-half of a quart of the potent, fiery liquor. A demitasse of strong Ethiopian coffee completes the spirit's demands. Satisfied, and without another word, he leaves the woman.

The older woman appears to become herself for about two minutes and then another zar, a female, enters her body. After a lengthy conversation with the zar in the zar tongue, Ayo orders coffee served to the woman for the benefit of her zar. With a final shriek, the zar leaves the woman.

After sitting rather calmly for a few minutes, the woman again begins to tremble and a third zar, a male, takes control of her. This spirit, speaking in an easily comprehensible voice, complains, "This woman has not brought me the trinkets and clothing which, during my last appearance, I ordered her to buy and to wear." Ayo reasons with the spirit, promising to remind the woman of the zar's order and to ask her brothers to help her with the purchase. The zar's final request for a flask of araqe is met. Content for the present, the zar departs. Following several less dramatic visitations by the zars of other people and a brief visit from the powerful zar of Ayo, the session ends and members of the congregation move homeward across the starlit fields.

ZAR AND THE INDIVIDUAL. To keep one's zar content, thus ending or preventing illness or misfortune caused by the zar, one must make offerings to him. At times an entire family instead of an individual makes offerings to a zar. Such a zar might belong to an important member of the family, for example the father or grandfather of those participating in the offering. Individual or group offerings to a zar may also be made to similar personal spirits described below. So-called medicine animals, that is, sheep or chickens with certain markings or colors, are sacrificed and are then usually consumed by the donor and his family and friends. Medicine animals may be specially bred for selection of their markings. If one of these animals, or its eggs or offspring, are sold, the money thus realized must be spent on a "gift" for the zar. Wearing new or colorful clothing and consuming alcoholic beverages are also considered "gifts" to one's zar.

Possession by spirits, like the practices of witchcraft and magic treated below, provides people with a release for their frustrations and tensions. In this way, an individual may redirect his hostilities from neighbors and kin, thereby avoiding physical or verbal strife which could lead to community disorganization if carried to an extreme. Thus, shamanism among the Qemant provides a social and psychological mechanism for maintenance of societal cohesion and preservation of the group.

A zar may verbalize a person's views concerning alleged injustices perpetrated against him (an insult or dispute over property) or it may express desires the gratification of which are forbidden (desired sexual unions) or not prudent (purchase or consumption of costly items). For example, if Bitaw's zar belittles an old antagonist or expresses interest in the robust daughter of a neighbor, Bitaw himself is not held responsible for the transgression, and community tranquility prevails. However, the antagonist may now be fully aware of Bitaw's viewpoint, and the neighbor's daughter may now act coquettish during a chance meeting on a community pathway. At times, a shaman who is sagaciously attuned to the gossip of the community will verbalize a client's thoughts in the presence of others: "I always go to Ayo, because his zar understands me and my desires."

Shamanism gives some social misfits an institution in which they can act out culturally acceptable roles and, additionally, this practice probably brings some measure of order and tranquility to the personalities of these people. Individuals who are deprived or rejected in some way, or who are apparently artless in most endeavors, find solace and a pleasurable social position in shamanism. Through shamanism, they receive attention, obtain material goods, sometimes acquire esteem, and are allowed to escape work ("She should labor lightly for one week to effect a cure of her ailment.") Thus, presents given and actions directed to one's zar are really intended for one's own pleasure and benefit, and the zar may be seen as part of an individual's personality, the conscious or unconscious expression of one's own wishes.

In the male-dominated society of the Qemant, a woman achieves some measure of security by succumbing to a zar and ailing until she receives affection or other compensation from her husband and his family with whom she resides for life. Indeed, a divorced woman or one whose husband is not amorous, or any woman denied or lacking interpersonal sexual outlets, is sometimes "afflicted" with an attentive male zar. Sexual deprivation of this nature apparently leads to physical or psychic autoeroticism. The pulsating movements of the body of a woman in the ecstatic trance of possession are sometimes said to result from her copulation with a zar, which, in this instance, may be considered an incubus—an evil spirit having sexual intercourse with a woman.

In all, rites associated with zars may generally be described as therapeutic, alleviating anxieties as well as providing gratifying affect. Gratifications available through beliefs in zars are not limited to opportunities to wear new clothing and to sate oneself with food and drink. The person who is possessed by a zar becomes the center of concern and may be looked upon with awe. The desire to indulge oneself and to draw attention to oneself may not be entirely overt. In his work on this phenomenon, Simon Messing states: "The 'zar' is a catch-all for many psychological disturbances, ranging from frustrated status ambition to actual mental illness." (1958:1125). Referring to self-indulgence, we may note that possession by the zars is not limited to times when shamanistic sessions are held. One may become possessed at any time, and possession often occurs on certain days when the zars are thought to be particularly active. Possession occurring at these times also provides much gratifying attention.

PERSONAL QOLE SPIRITS. Although not everyone has a zar, everyone is said to have a guardian spirit, generally referred to as *yeqole* [my (guardian) spirit]. Personal qoles are far less powerful than the qoles described in Chapter 4 as genii loci and have little in common with them except that they are both invisible supernatural beings. Personal qoles rarely possess people, but should they turn malevolent or otherwise become bothersome, a shaman may be consulted to handle them.

Knowing that one's personal qole is present eases tensions of all kinds, as the qole is said to insure well-being. Erada says, "A person without one of these spirits is a person without a protector." Qoles can also predict future events. For example, Adonech once stated that her qole made the fire in the hearth burn in a certain manner, thus telling her that my assistant and I were coming to visit her family on that day.

Although a personal qole is usually benevolent, or at least neutral, it might become malevolent at times, especially if it is not occasionally honored by sacrifices. Some qoles remain benevolent without receiving any offerings. An individual or an entire family may make offerings honoring these spirits. However, some informants claimed that one sacrifice precipitates another because the spirit develops "a habit of hunger." Thus, if possible, one should not begin to make offerings to one of these spirits unless it is causing misfortune.

After Erada and his family make a sacrifice to a qole, or other personal spirit, they customarily remain inside their houses for three days. They must not meet with other people and at most are allowed to communicate with others by shouting to them from a distance. On the morning of the third day, the women clean their houses, and the men bury the uneaten remains of the sacrifice, thereby preventing dogs from eating the remains and thus angering the spirit. As is usual, but not mandatory, each member of the family then anoints his or her hair with butter and regular activities are resumed.

There are specific names for guardian qoles of which the two most common are *wuqabi* and *tayaz* (also called *taz*). Most people say that the two spirits are the same, and I could discern no difference between the two from information given to me by informants. In fact, the wuqabi and tayaz may once have been distinct personal spirits of the Agaw, but the two have coalesced to the extent that the only thing distinct about them today is their names. The wuqabi-tayaz is also acknowledged as a guardian spirit by the Amhara and Falasha. Ethiopians are familiar with the Arabian jinn but this spirit is rare in Qemantland.

Occasionally, an active guardian spirit makes a person so ill that he is not able to leave his house. In such a case, a balazar may make a house call, carrying with him his shamanistic role equipment. Ayo's most acute case of this nature involved a man who had experienced fever and aches in his body for over a week. Suspecting his tayaz as the source of the trouble, the man's family summons Ayo who first states his fee—two silver dollars for this first house call and one silver dollar for any subsequent calls. The family agrees.

With the anguished members of the family looking over his shoulder, among them women sighing and lamenting, Ayo sits down on a stool next to the bed of his patient. His bedside manner, starting with a tattoo on the drum, is very reassuring. Then, Ayo begins to rock back and forth, chanting and masticating chat leaves wadded in his cheek. Suddenly, the music stops as Ayo shudders and appears to go into a quiet trance for about twenty minutes. Recovering, Ayo says he has spoken to his patient's tayaz, who is agitated because he has been forgotten. To soothe the spirit, the shaman prescribes and gives to the man *awza*, a medicine made of honey, chat, and water boiled together. The shaman also instructs the family to gather a local wild root and to boil it in water for the patient. "Its brew will ease the pain," he asserts. Next, Ayo chews some fresh chat and blows the juice over his patient. This act is supposed to make the tayaz speak. However, the ill man simply lies quietly upon his bed. Further chanting and beating of the drum by Ayo fails to induce possession of the man by his tayaz.

Finally, Ayo decides to try to enter into an oral contract with the tayaz later that night. He then asks the tayaz not to bother the peasant and promises that the peasant will reciprocate by occasionally wearing new white clothing, by sacrificing a medicine chicken, by promising further sacrifices in the future, and by continuing to consult with the balazar. "With such acts," Ayo tells his patient, "it is probable that the spirit will not bring further grief to you, but it may return once a year or so." I might add that the man recovered gradually during the following week, and that he was quite thankful to Ayo for the cure and for the peace of mind the balazar had brought to him upon his sickbed.

Some of the plants in Ayo's pharmacopoeia ease a patient's discomfort, and a few actually give relief from some ailments (for example, stomach disorders); others induce hallucinations or aid in bringing on possession; many are ineffective. Nevertheless, all of Ayo's curing activities are satisfying to the Qemant, a people whose limited technology has very few means of coping with the specters of disease and illness found in their world. In the time of disorder wrought by illness there is a need to do something, and something is done when Ayo, the shaman, takes charge and begins to restore order to a small segment of the capricious universe. Through the power of suggestion, Ayo induces good mental health into an ill person, girding his patient for combat against organic disease and helping negate the effect of psychosomatic disease. If he should fail to cure a patient, Ayo has an abundance of excuses, including an implacable zar, improperly mixed medicine, and an incorrectly executed rite. Therefore, when a person dies from a disease, Qemant do not question the validity of shamanism or the power of the shaman.

SPECIFIC SPIRITS OF DISEASE.   Among the Qemant, Amhara, and Falasha, disease and all instances of death other than physical—as opposed to supernatural —homicide are attributed to supernatural causes, usually spirits and the evil eye. While personal spirits may bring illness to a person, specific spirits of disease may cause illness of epidemic proportions to befall an entire community. These spirits of disease apparently have no other function.

When a community is afflicted with a specific spirit of disease, it may hold a procession called *baseta masanat* (seeing off of the disease) to carry away the pestilence. The procession is an effective mechanism to reduce anxiety from disease, allowing a community to act against the capricious and deadly spirits that cause sickness. I observed such a procession late in 1964 after an epidemic of malaria in the province of Bagemder. The procession originated in Balasa, southeast of Gondar, and moved along the trail toward Matama, on the Sudanese border, via Saqalt and Chelga. The thirty people in the procession were collectively transporting the spirit of malaria that had caused the epidemic in Balasa. Each person carried a piece of a pottery vessel or a piece of a gourd containing the spirit. When they reached a new area, the people in the procession handed the pieces of containers to people in the new area who, in turn, carried them to another area. Members of the procession were Amhara, Qemant, or Falasha, depending on the location of the communities involved. Since the spirit of disease could have "given birth" (caused an epidemic) at any stop of the procession, each community was eager to carry the spirit on to the neighboring community.

The Qemant also hold a similar procession to counteract outbreaks of smallpox. They travel from the center of the disease in the community to the main trail. Upon reaching the trail, the people consume food and drink brought with them, carefully leaving part of the food and drink at the trail for the spirit. Hopefully, the spirit will not return to their community.

Witchcraft, Magic, and Divination

The Qemant, all other Agaw, and the Amhara believe in and practice three supernatural adaptations to the environment—witchcraft, magic, and divination. They believe that these three forms of supernaturalism give them some measure of control over their social and physical worlds and that the third form allows a limited perception of future events. The Qemant also use the three forms of supernaturalism to defuse potentially explosive situations, by providing outlets for hostilities and tensions, and to supply explanations not available through empirical means. For example, using supernaturalism, a peasant secretly curses an antagonist instead of striking him and seeks answers to his questions regarding failure of his crops or illness in his family. In both instances the peasant has the satisfaction of taking some immediate action in situations where naturalistic thought and behavior are difficult or impossible.

Witchcraft may be considered as the power within a person to project evil psychically. Witches are often females, but may also be male. Although witchcraft is an inherent capability, the power may be dormant, sporadic, or even unrealized by the possessor. Such persons can project their evil over great distances, can transform themselves into various kinds of weremammals, and can blight things with a glance (evil eye) or a word (evil tongue). While witchcraft is used to account for unexpected events otherwise having no evidence supporting an explanation, there is usually some evidence for the perpetration of magical happenings.

Magic is not a "built in," or inner, power as is witchcraft. It is a set of learned rites, involving incantations and materials generally known as "medicine," performed to manipulate the environment in order to achieve a desired end in the social or physical worlds. Magic may be good (white) or evil (black or sorcerous) and should not be confused with varieties of sleight-of-hand entertainment in the Western world. Nevertheless, religious practitioners of all kinds may use sleight-of-hand in their rites just as they may use ventriloquism, spirit posession, or incomprehensible ritual speech.

Divination is the supernatural practice of being able to perceive, to some extent, future happenings or unknown information. There are two kinds of divination: shamanistic, in which inspiration from supernatural beings is sought, and magical, in which omens are magically interpreted.

Shamanism, the roles of the priests in formal religion, and the three forms of supernaturalism covered in this section are not mutually exclusive. There is no clear-cut distinction between the various activities of supernatural practitioners. Many priests—but not the Qemant priests—and shamans may practice witchcraft, magic, and divination, or magicians may additionally practice divination, or a person may be simply a magician, witch, or diviner.

HUNTING FOR A WITCH. It is difficult to find a witch in Qemantland. Few people, Qemant or otherwise, consciously play the role of a witch as they do the roles of shaman, magician, and diviner. However, the role of a witch is part of the reference group that Qemant and others relate to for guides to behavior; that is, people act and think as though witches do exist. People suspect others of being witches and believe they have felt the effects of witchcraft, even though no one admits to being a witch or perpetrating the associated blight on men, animals, plants, and events. In order to place the blame for one's misfortune or, sometimes, to make an excuse for one's inept actions or errors in judgment, a witch is hunted and sought out as a scapegoat. Usually a person in a distant community, but sometimes a neighbor, may be accused of witchcraft when a vexed person tries to find the cause of an event in terms of another person's malevolence.

The Qemant and their neighbors believe in psychic projections of evil, especially evil eye, evil tongue, and evil thought. These three projections constitute the major forms of witchcraft in the Qemant region, and Agaw and Amhara often say these varieties are used when someone envies another's possessions or good fortune. A person causing misfortune to befall another person by looking with a covetous eye at him or his property is called a *buda* (evil-eyed one). Any person of any ethnic group of Ethiopia may be accused of being a buda. In most instances the evil-eyed person is said to be from an ethnic group other than one's own, but it is possible for a witch to be found within one's own group. Amhara usually say Falasha are budas and sometimes say Qemant are; Qemant usually say Falasha are budas. The Falasha are thought to have the evil eye and to turn nocturnally into hyenas which devour human corpses, especially victims of evil eye, because they practice blacksmithing and pottery making, crafts abhorred by Qemant and Amhara alike. Fear by the Qemant of being bewitched by someone from another ethnic group minimizes contacts with "them," the outsiders, and fosters intragroup familiarization with "us," fellow Qemant.

The enmity between ethnic groups associated with their fear and suspicion of witchcraft was made clear to me one dark night when I was lost in a Falasha community located close to Amhara and Qemant areas. I was finally able to find two Falasha men who were willing to guide me over the hills for a short distance; then, suddenly, they hesitated to go any further. After much persuasion and an offer of Eth. $1.00 (considered two day's pay in rural areas), they took me a little further, until they came to the boundary separating the Falasha area from that of · the Qemant and Amhara. At this juncture, they absolutely refused to go any further, and the Eth. $10.00 I produced did not change their minds. The reason was soon made clear to me. If the Falasha guides crossed over the boundary, the Amhara or Qemant, thinking the Falasha were about to devour a corpse or to bewitch someone, would accuse them of being budas and would inflict some kind of mayhem upon their persons. Obviously, I had lost my guides and I stumbled off in the dark on my own.

Martin Flad, the nineteenth century missionary, noted the association of food and the evil eye in Abyssinia, an association that has changed little since his time. Flad states that a woman prepares food in the dark recess of the house for fear of the evil eye of strangers and that any mishap relating to food occurring in the presence of a stranger is laid to his evil eye. He continues:

> Abyssinians [Amhara and Agaw] never carry any food or medicine uncovered for fear of the shadow [evil eye]. They take their meals in the strictest privacy; a covering is then hung before the door, in spite of the darkness, and it would be considered the most flagrant breach of courtesy to intrude upon a family at mealtimes (1869:13–14).

Here we have an instance where we can use the accounts of early travelers in Ethiopia (surveyed in Chapter 1) to determine to what extent certain elements of Ethiopian culture are changing or remaining stable.

A more diffuse variety of evil eye, easily used by almost anyone, is *aynmawgat* (eye piercing), meaning the blighting of a person or object by looking at them in strong envy. The envy is expressed in thought only. In and around Qemantland almost anyone can project witchlike qualities at times. Another kind of psychic projection is *melas* (tongue), the process of blighting a person or object by looking at them and then praising them aloud. Anyone may also do this. A person who blights things in this manner, or is thought to do this, is called *tequr melas* (literally, black tongue). A third psychic projection, used less frequently than the other two, is *mansat* (literally, lift up, but better translated, to think ill of a person), evil thought by a group against someone who creates tension in the community. This person might be agitating for rights to another's land or otherwise disturbing harmony in the community. Mansat is more overt than other psychic projections of evil; the people explicitly want to be rid of the troublemaker. It is said that those who suffer mansat will die or at least become ill. If the person dies under these conditions, people say, "Mansat killed him."

CASTING A SPELL. In the Qemant region, magic is practiced by all shamans, by certain knowledgeable peasants of any ethnic group, and by some religious practitioners of the Christian and Muslim faiths. Beneficial, or white, magic is often used to counteract the effects of malevolent, or black, magic and witchcraft. For example, various magical means are used to ward off the effects of the evil eye. To protect cattle, the trailing edges of their ears are notched while the cattle are young; to protect crops, skulls of cattle on poles, or several poles made from limbs or small trees from which the bark has been peeled, are placed upright in the fields. No reason could be found for these actions except that they were "known to be effective."

To safeguard oneself against black magic, Qemant, Falasha, and Amhara wear amulets as protection against malevolent spirits and other forms of evil. Amulets are charms with protective functions and are made by magicians. In the Qemant area, amulets consist of small pieces of inscribed parchment placed in a small leather case that is worn around the neck on a cord. As a neck pendant, the case is regarded as decorative. The parchment is inscribed in Geez or Arabic with mixed characters or with phrases from the Bible or Koran. Figures and geometric designs may be included. It is not just the sacred phrases which protect a person but also the magic of writing. The Ethiopian peasants are illiterate rather than nonliterate. They well know that letters exist and their respect for writing approaches veneration. Except for these amulets, no forms of talismans are used by the Qemant. Indeed, they have no other sacred manmade objects or relics of any kind.

When sorcerers (black magicians) practice their dark arts, they may at times use empirical means, such as drugs or physical acts of destruction, but usually they rely upon their incantatory spells, to which objects of medicine have been adroitly added. This latter method has been used against Erada. For example, when one antagonist wishes misfortune to befall Erada, he purchases some "medicine" eggs from a sorcerer. Chanting and gesturing over the eggs, the sorcerer guarantees to bring misfortune to anyone upon whose premises the foul eggs are buried. When darkness falls and Erada's dogs are asleep, the antagonist buries the eggs near Erada's homestead. The next day, Erada excavates the fresh burial and, as soon as possible, goes before the council of elders, excitedly asking them to maledict the unknown foe.

Erada has strong reason to be agitated. He knows that black magic, like other forms of malevolent supernaturalism, is dangerous. Not only does Erada believe misfortune results from these practices but he has actually seen people become sick and grievously ill after they were openly cursed or put under a sorcerer's spell. A personality believing in supernatural cause and effect may inflict psychosomatic maladies upon the body. This phenomenon is sometimes labeled by anthropologists as "voodoo death," especially if it runs its full, fatal course. Knowledge of harmful supernaturalism stimulates fear in the personality which galvanizes the body for a fearsome emergency that never comes. The readiness of the body for emergency continues until the person enters shock, a condition complicated by loss of the vital desire to eat and drink. Erada, of course, does not know of and would not believe in the mental and physiological occurrence just outlined. All Erada knows is that sorcery can be a cause of very perilous events in his world.

Erada believes he is quite pragmatic about the action he takes to settle the entire affair. Given the limitations set by the technology and scientific knowledge extant in his culture, Erada is indeed quite rational in his perception of his plight and in what he proposes to do about it. When Erada wants to buy a pot, he goes to a potter; to mend a broken iron tool, he goes to the blacksmith; to avert the spell of a sorcerer, he goes to a supernatural practitioner. Erada decides to consult a shaman. As luck would have it, there is one in the family. His younger brother Ayo, the zar-master, will give ardent attention to Erada's plight and will charge frugal Erada only a modest or token fee. Ayo uses incantations and medicines of white magic to counter the sorcerous effect of the sinister eggs. Actually, he is neutralizing the effect of the eggs upon his brother's mind. In the meantime, the council of elders withholds its curse until they have a more accurately defined human target for malediction. Perhaps Erada's assailant feared that the council would curse him on behalf of the community, or maybe he was impressed by Ayo's magic, but, in any case, he did not strike again.

DIVINING TOMORROW'S NEWS TODAY. Like almost everyone else, the Qemant are interested in learning what tomorrow will bring; most people are curious and therefore enjoy a "tip" on the ups and downs of life in the future. To elicit this information, various divinatory practices are used by laymen and religious practitioners. Through divination, the Qemant feel a little less anxious and a little more secure in their sociocultural and physical world.

When Bitaw, Erada's son, begins a trip outside of his community, he listens for certain personal names along the way. Names we would translate as Happy, Wealthy, and Light symbolize good fortune and a successful and safe journey. Hearing the names of or meeting people with names like Broken, Take-from, Very-strong, or Hold-him indicate bad fortune and will cause Bitaw to return home. Nagash, Bitaw's brother, does not believe in the above omens as much as Bitaw does and would not have let any of the names influence the course of his journey. However, Nagash does believe, as others do, that meeting two people coming toward him predicts good fortune, as does meeting a person with a full container. Encountering a person with an empty container forebodes misfortune.

Certain people in Qemantland have greater skills in divination than the average layman. Shamans, through inspiration from their zars, can often forecast future events or uncover hidden information. Still other people are solely diviners and may predict certain future events from flights of birds whose language they claim to understand.

A female shaman in Qemantland, who is a competitor of Ayo, is said to have uncovered hidden information as the result of a test given to her by a regional Amhara feudal official. The official is said to have hidden a rifle from his chief servants, who were to find its hiding place from information given to them by the zar of the lady balazar. The shaman and her spirit apparently received a grade of "A" on the test from the official, for he gave her the rifle as a reward for discovering its place of concealment. Such stories are recounted by the score in Qemantland.

I conclude with an ethnographic note. In a conversation with a missionary from a highly industralized and literate Western nation carrying on his work in Ethiopia, I learned that the people of northcentral Ethiopia were mistaken in their beliefs concerning zar. The missionary emphatically stated that zar spirits do not possess these poor people—Satan does. To this day the missionary endeavors diligently to exorcise Satan from the bodies of the afflicted. This places the supernaturalism examined in this chapter in perspective. The Western reader can empathize with the Qemant when he realizes that some of his own traditions are not too different from theirs.

6

Political Organization

I N EARLIEST TIMES, the Qemant probably vested supreme political power in individual patriarchs of the clans, like the nine Keber culture heroes (see Fig. 1), especially during periods of war or other general social disorder. In times of peace, power reverted to more democratic control. Sometime before 1600, the Qemant became politically subordinate to the feudal hierarchy of the Amhara. However, the Qemant were never a military threat to the Amhara, who therefore paid little attention to Qemant political organization and allowed them considerable autonomy. The Imperial Abyssinian Chronicles and the oral history of the Qemant make no mention of any Qemant reaction against Amhara, and legends of the Qemant depict their warriors as being under Amhara leadership.

Continued semiautonomy of the native political structure, which had broad judicial functions, enabled the Qemant to serve as their own corrective instrument in seeking out and punishing those who deviated from the cultural norms. Thus, group identity and social cohesion were maintained for several centuries. During the period of enforced Amharization of the 1880s the religion of the Qemant was weakened, and because of the intimate relation that existed between politics and religion, the traditional political structure was thus also weakened. Bonds of group identity and ideas of exclusiveness lost strength. Although not enforced by imperial mandate, rapid Amharization began at this time and has continued ever since.

The administrative power of the Qemant seems to have varied for some centuries after the Amhara became dominant, and it was undoubtedly inversely proportionate to the power exercised at the moment by the feudal administrators. The Amhara maintained a position of political dominance at all times, but they allowed the Qemant great autonomy in judicial matters. This autonomy posed no threat to the Amhara, and the Qemant were permitted, in fact, to resolve their legal problems entirely within the context of their own politicoreligious organization. Authority allowed to the Qemant in matters other than judiciary has, however, always been limited.

As in former times, the Qemant delegate and exercise power in a basically democratic manner. Most administrative and judicial affairs are settled on the lowest level by councils of elders. Matters not resolved by the councils of elders are referred to an intermediate level of political power in the persons of certain priests and secular officials. Final arbiters in the Qemant political structure are the wambars, particularly the two superior wambars of Chelga and Karkar.

Councils of Elders

Councils of elders are the basic units of authority among the Qemant. The councils are democratic assemblies composed of males who are "old enough to have gray hair" and who usually have a moderate amount of prestige. Elders who do most of the debating and have the greatest voice in making decisions are those who have undergone the rite of *kasa*, marking transition to the esteemed status of venerable elder. This special status signifies marked closeness to Mezgana (God). Although the rite of kasa is not required for all elders, the councils of elders are closely integrated with the religion.

Most administrative and judicial matters affecting the daily lives of the members of each Qemant community are deliberated and settled by the councils of elders without recourse to the Amhara, thus helping to maintain cohesiveness in Qemant society. The opinions of members of the Keber moiety were formerly held to be the more important in council deliberations. This bias, and the fact that priests and wambars are elected from certain "priestly" families, gave an oligarchic tendency to the otherwise generally democratic government. However, the position of superiority of members of the Keber moiety has disappeared during the last forty years, and the oligarchic tendency has thus become less pronounced.

FORMAL AND INFORMAL COUNCILS. There are two types of councils, formal and informal. Meetings of the formal councils are held as a part of the monthly meetings of the principal association (*mahebar*) of a Qemant community. (Membership, recruitment, and functions of associations are discussed in Chapter 7.) At meetings of the formal council, elders present judicial and administrative problems for discussion and decision. An annually elected leader (*alaka*), whose only compensation is prestige, presides over the formal council. He channels complaints and litigation brought before him to subcouncils, which he creates, as the need arises, from elders of the community. Subcouncils are made up of a leader and five or more members, allowing almost every Qemant male to participate sometime during his life in the government of his community. Subcouncils report their findings to the formal council, which then decides the course of action.

Informal councils of elders are ad hoc bodies, performing only judicial functions, formed at the request of two litigants who personally choose five to seven council members and a leader.

Investigations and deliberations by formal councils and their subcouncils and by informal councils cover many months, sometimes several years. The time required for litigation helps preserve community tranquility; during this period,

Formal council of elders conferring on a two-year-old dispute over land. Note long sticks carried by all men often used to ward off dogs.

neither litigant resorts to physical strife because each feels that the council will eventually vindicate him to some extent.

LITIGATION. Because he is an older male and has undergone the rite of kasa, Erada belongs to a formal council and often heads informal councils. During my fieldwork, I observed Erada and other elders performing their duties as council members. A typical litigation adjudicated by Erada and other members of a formal council concerned the sale to a young man of a horse belonging to an aged peasant:

On an appointed meeting day, the bearded, gray-haired elders, clad in togas, walk across the fields and assemble in a cleared area between the roots of two large trees. While the council members repose with vessels of beer under the canopy of trees, the council leader arranges for a guarantor, selected from assembled kith and kin, for each of the litigants. Any fines to be levied pass through the guarantor, who is responsible for payment. Erada and the other council members then hear evidence in separate hearings from each party to the dispute. This action prevents disruption of the judicial procedure arising from arguments between litigants and their witnesses.

From the hearings, the council members learn that last year the young man paid the older man Eth. $16.00, an advance two-thirds payment for the horse. The older man had decided to keep the horse until the final payment was made. When the young man had saved the remaining eight dollars of the purchase price of Eth. $24.00, he offered the money to the old peasant who then professed no knowledge of the original transaction. Following many weeks of meetings covering several hours each week, Erada and the other elders present their decision to the litigants: "The old man must return the money or complete the transaction." As often happens, the older peasant refuses to accept the council's judgment. When either litigant refuses to accept a decision (an unaccepted judgment is not binding), the elders hold additional hearings leading to further deliberations.

The old man becomes recalcitrant, refusing to attend further hearings, now being held without him. For many months, the council requests the old man to appear, but he is adamant. Finally, the council decides to invoke their customary sanction. The old man receives a message stating, "Appear before council or we will curse you." This malediction is effected by pouring a sacred beer (*meski*) onto the earth in the name of the accursed one. Rather than receive the ultimate punishment, the old man finally agrees to come to court and, finally, to complete the transaction—for two dollars more than the original purchase price.

As is customary when a litigant finally accepts a judgment, partially or wholly against him, the old man places a stone on the back of his neck, bows to the younger man, and says, "Pardon me." The other litigant thereupon reciprocates with precisely the same ritual. The two then kiss one another on both cheeks and are blessed by Erada and the other elders of the council. This blessing is especially valuable since many of the elders have received the rite of kasa.

Other litigations handled that year by Erada and the council included several disputes over rights to use of land and a preponderance of cases concerning the exact boundaries of neighbors' fields. (At times boundary fences mysteriously move several feet during the night.) Other particular cases centered around the killing of a man's dog and the disappearance of sixty trees from a plot of land far removed from the owner's house. Some men sought compensation for insults and others wanted compensation for breach of oral contract. Should a matter remain unsettled after protracted litigation before a council of elders, it will be referred to higher levels of authority within the Qemant politicoreligious organization. However, Qemant prefer to have matters settled by the councils. To illustrate this sentiment Erada quotes the proverb: "One piece of wood will not burn; one judge cannot decide."

CHRISTIAN QEMANT AND THEIR COUNCILS. Among the Christian Qemant both forms of the traditional council are retained. Meetings of the formal councils among the Christian Qemant are now held on one or two Sundays of each month and are part of the meetings of an association called *sanbate* (Sunday association). Elders deliberate under two leaders, annually elected, who are called *afaliq* and *wambarliq*. Both have the same duties and power. The rite of kasa has no relevance to the status of elders among Christian Qemant, and the influence of religion in the activities of the councils of Christian Qemant is less important than among the pagan-Hebraic Qemant.

However, in some communities of Christian Qemant, the transition from the pagan-Hebraic hierarchy of officialdom to full acceptance of the Amhara feudal hierarchy has not been complete. The councils of elders have made some adjustments in the customary modes of enforcing decisions, but much remains that is native Qemant. For example, people in one Qemant community which has been Christian for at least ten years go to the community's sacred grove to enforce decisions of its councils of elders. Here, the people direct prayers to Mezgana, asking him to punish any person who will not give the redress demanded in a judgment against him. If this person is eventually punished by misfortune sent by Mezgana, or if he repents and gives compensation to the plaintiff, the plaintiff goes to the grove and makes a sacrificial offering of an animal, which is consumed by the elders of the community. Among all Christian Qemant, the ultimate punishment levied by the council of elders is to pour beer onto the ground while the Sunday association curses the malefactor. This custom is derived from rites of malediction of the pagan-Hebraic Qemant, in which the sacred beer, *meski*, is used.

The judicial role of the council of elders in communities of Qemant is much greater then the judicial role of the council of elders of the sanbate association also found in communities of Christian Amhara. Christian Qemant still try to settle disputes themselves without resort to the Amhara feudal officials. This practice gives a feeling of unity and also serves in moderate measure to maintain a boundary between the Christian Qemant and the Amhara. It seems certain, however, that in the next few decades the Christian Qemant will become totally Amharized.

THE COUNCILS AND THE OUTSIDE WORLD. Qemant councils of elders also have some authority in matters that concern relations with the world outside Qemant society. Among matters they debate and decide upon are relations of the community with the Amhara, such as arranging to provide required corvee labor for maintenance of trails, and the question of whether or not to allow foreign missionaries to enter the community. Councils also initiate projects such as the construction of additions to a meeting place or the forging of a new trail.

Intermediate Political Positions

In former times, the lower priests (*abayegariyas*) and especially the higher priests (*kamazanas*), who are Kebers, had larger political roles than they hold today. At present, while nominally able to hear cases and settle disputes, the priests seldom do more than advise on matters that relate to preserving tranquility in the community. However, they assist the wambar in judicial matters.

At present, most judicial duties on the intermediate level are performed by the wambar's spokesman, the *afaliq*. The afaliq is selected from members of the Keber moiety by the wambar, who also compensates this part-time administrator. Only a man who is acceptable to the members of his own community is chosen to serve as an afaliq.

In the past, afaliqs traveled across the country to settle litigation and to see that the laymen and the priests observed Qemant laws. The afaliq had authority to levy punishments, which were most commonly fines; however, the Qemant could remember no case when an afaliq actually exercised his authority over a priest. Each wambar had several afaliqs, but since the number of pagan-Hebraic Qemant has sharply declined, there has been no need to fill positions that fall vacant. Cases or matters not settled by an afaliq are referred to the wambar.

The Wambar as the Final Arbiter

Besides his role as head of the Qemant priesthood, the wambar has judicial and leadership roles. Disputes not settled by councils of elders or by officials in intermediate political positions are referred to a wambar. Before the period of enforced Amharization there were two superior wambars, one residing in Karkar and one in Chelga. Further, there were ten or more lesser wambars, residing in various other Qemant communities, who, if they were west of Guwang River, were subordinate to the wambar of Chelga and, if they were east of this river, were subordinate to the wambar of Karkar. The subordinate wambars settled most disputes referred to them, and passed only the most difficult cases on to their respective superior wambars. After the turn of the century, only the two superior wambars remained. Of the two superior wambars, the one in Karkar was paramount and was often referred to as the "great wambar." After the death of the wambar of Karkar in 1955, no one succeeded him, and the superior wambar of Chelga is today the only wambar of the Qemant.

STANDING BEFORE THE WAMBAR. A wambar usually hears a dispute jointly with the higher and lower priests of a local community. All three participate, interrogating the plaintiff and the defendant and, finally, making the decision. However, the wambar has the final word in decisions. Each party to a dispute, including supporters and witnesses, is heard separately and is admonished that Mezgana will punish any person who is lying. The plaintiff and the defendant must each post a bond of a stated amount of livestock, cloth, or grain. Whoever loses the case forfeits his bond to the wambar, who receives part of his income therefrom.

In cases where evidence is not conclusive or where stories from opposing sides balance one another, the two parties are taken to the local sacred grove. Under the wambar's direction, the priests give the defendant a new axe and sickle of iron. (Qemant ordinarily use sickles only for the purpose of reaping.) The accused man must use the tools to chop down one of the trees in the sacred grove. As he chops, he must say aloud, "If I am guilty, let Mezgana chop me into pieces as I chop this tree." If the man is actually guilty, his fear of super-natural punishment causes him to confess before he touches the tools. If innocent, he need have no fear of felling the sacred tree, as the penalty of the conditional curse is transferred from him to the false plaintiff. If the plaintiff confesses that he has borne false witness or if the accused confesses guilt before he takes up the tools, any fine or penalty is automatically cut in half.

Upon reaching a decision, the wambar levies fines or punishments, returns property to the rightful owners, or, in disputes over land, assigns the rights to the land to its legal recipient. For minor infractions of religious regulations (sins), the wambar levies such punishments as sleeping on the bare ground for seven nights, drinking a strong purge called *koso* for seven days, and daily washing of the body with water drawn daily. As a further part of the punishment, persons found guilty of sins must give the wambar two bars of salt. Sins include allowing oneself or causing sacred ground to become ritually polluted, irreverence to members of the priesthood or pantheon, and not observing holy days in the proper manner.

The wambar preserves Qemant mores with awesome punishments that reach beyond the grave and bar the way to heaven. Curses and ostracism are the ultimate punishments handed out by a wambar, and they are ordinarily levied only if someone challenges his authority. For example, if a person does not abide by a wambar's decision, or if he violates a major religious rule, such as marrying outside Qemant religious laws, he is ostracized. Ostracism is complete and final and continues after death. An ostracized person receives no funeral and no rite of passage into heaven.

HOMICIDE AND THE WAMBAR.   The most serious judicial matter to reach a wambar is a killing. Qemant law does not recognize accidental death or manslaughter; to take another person's life is to murder him. The dictum of "an eye for an eye" is Qemant law, and the penalty for taking another's life is for the killer to lose his own life at the hands of the dead man's kin. The killer has only one recourse: He may pay blood money to the family of the person he has killed. Fifty years ago the indemnity was around eighty Maria Theresa dollars, but it is now at least Eth. $400 and may run as high as Eth. $700 to Eth. $1000.

If the family of the killer cannot come to an agreement with the family of the deceased through councils or other intermediaries, the wambar takes up the problem. If agreement is reached by both parties on the amount of indemnity, an oral contract is made with the help of the wambar or council of elders. This contract is then presented by both parties to the Amhara officials, who levy an additional fine upon the guilty person and confiscate any weapon used in the killing. In this way the Amhara validate Qemant judgments in cases of homicide. After the contract is fulfilled and the fine is paid, the killer cannot be punished further.

Until recently, any cases involving Qemant that came to the attention of Amhara administrators were sent to the wambar of Chelga or of Karkar. The wambar informed the Amhara of his decision and disposition of the case. Today, if a judgment of blood indemnity is disputed, the case may be referred to the Amhara judges and administrators. If the Amhara officials do not settle the case, as happens occasionally, the kin of the deceased take the life of the killer. In keeping with the idea of blood vengeance, an endless chain of vendetta may then ensue, but this rarely happens. The policy of the Ethiopian government is to try to punish for killings, thus preventing vendettas.

THE WEALTH OF THE WAMBAR. In addition to the authority conferred upon him by priesthood, a wambar gains authority from wealth coming from contributions to ceremonies, forfeited bonds, and fines for infractions of religious laws. The wambar also receives two bars of salt or two Maria Theresa silver dollars for each personal ceremony. Such ceremonies are sanctioned by a wambar but conducted by the priests and include rites of passage, ordination of members of the priesthood, and, until very recently, confirmation of local appointments of the lowest of feudal officials, the *cheqa shum* (roughly equivalent to the medieval English sheriff). In the last century, the wambar of Karkar received tribute from communities in the eastern half of the Qemant area, and the wambar of Chelga received tribute from communities in the western half. This system of taxation ended in the area around Karkar with the advent of enforced Amharization during the 1880s and in the area around Chelga by the 1920s.

A major source of a wambar's wealth is the agricultural yield of land that is worked for him. The power and prestige of a wambar allow him to successfully claim rights to use large amounts of land, far larger than a peasant may claim and too large to be cultivated by one family. Having activated dormant use rights to land, the wambar cultivates the land with corvee, which requires each adult male in the wambar's domain to provide three days of labor annually.

7

Social Organization

THE QEMANT, like other people of preindustrial regions, are united by a web of kinship not markedly recognized or used in the interactions of industrialized people like the Yankees of North America. In peasant and primitive societies, a person's existence and well-being ultimately depend upon the maintenance of complex links which, when traced through a network of kinship, unite this person with a multitude of relatives. Sometimes, as we shall see among the Qemant, a person with a rather limited kinship network may additionally unite himself with others by fictionalizing kinship links through contracts of reciprocity with those to whom he is otherwise unrelated. Still other Qemant social contracts unite groups of people into associations dedicated to the welfare of members of these groups.

The social organization of the Qemant examined in this chapter may, at first glance, seem complex and perhaps even cumbersome. However, the reader should realize that this social organization, like the non-Indo-European langauge and thought patterns of the Qemant, seems unwieldly to us at first because we are not familiar with it. The Qemant web of kinship is a flexible and economical system of sociocultural elements used to facilitate interpersonal relations. The Qemant kinship network is one of their adaptations to their environment.

Unilineal Organization of Kin

The probable existence of a pagan-Hebraic religion among the Qemant is alluded to in the literature on Ethiopia, and finding such a religion was, therefore, no surprise to me. However, finding elements of unilineal descent among the Qemant, including a dual organization into moieties,[1] was unexpected, es-

---

[1] The kinship terms used in this section are defined in the subsection of Chapter 1 entitled "Integrative Factors."

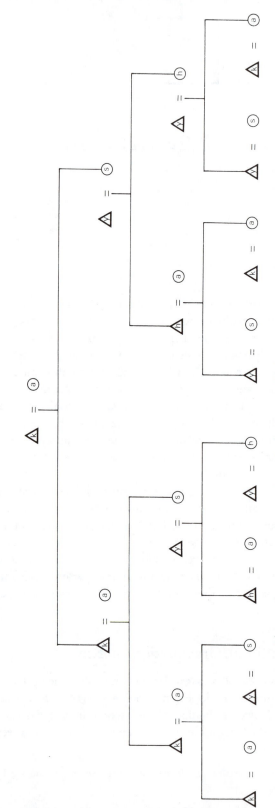

Fig. 2. Qemant marriage rules: K: Keber (a Keber moiety member in general);
Y: Yetanti (a Yetanti moiety member in general); k: keber (a male Keber moiety
member); y: yetanti (a male Yetanti moiety member, "son of a Yetanti's son");
s: senkra (female Keber moiety member, the daughter of a keber); h: senkraybura
(a Yetanti moiety member, the child of a senkra); a: amazti (Yetanti moiety member, the daughter of a yetanti).

pecially since no traces of this type of social organization are evident among the other Agaw and the Amhara and Tegre. The only hint of unilineal organization among the Qemant is found in a statement by Martin Flad: "[T]he Qemants are divided into two parties, the superior call themselves 'KEBERTI' and the inferior 'YETANTI'" (1866:20–21).

PATRIMOIETIES AND MARRIAGE. All Qemant are either Keber (the -ti, if it ever existed, is not used today) or Yetanti. These two moieties, which are not territorially defined, are closely integrated with the pagan-Hebraic religion and are not important among Qemant who have been Christian for over a generation. Descent in the Keber and Yetanti moieties and in their component clans is reckoned patrilineally. Membership in a moiety determines eligibility for positions in the priesthood.

Each moiety is exogamous. If a Keber marries Keber or a Yetanti marries Yetanti, the act is considered incestuous and would be "like marrying your own sister," according to the son of the late wambar of Karkar. Rules of marriage do not, however, follow simple lines of moiety division; for details of rules see Fig. 2. Strict adherence to moiety exogamy safeguards the strict societal endogamy of the Qemant. As mentioned earlier, members of the priesthood rigorously enforce the marriage rules with terrible punishments that reach beyond the grave to bar the way to heaven. Since no one wants to violate the marriage rules, non-Qemant never enter and, until very recently, Qemant never left the closely knit society through marriage. Thus the dual organization and associated marriage rules, as safeguarded by the wambar and his priests, provide a strong boundary-maintaining mechanism. Marriage among the Qemant is monogamous. Concubinage exists, but there is now no polygyny, although Qemant legends, Ethiopic manuscripts, and early European accounts mention this practice.

Every Qemant, male or female, is designated in a general way as either a "Keber" or a "Yetanti." However, when it is useful to designate the sex and exact status of a person, all Keber males are specifically called "keber"; also, many Yetanti males are specifically called "yetanti," but only if they are "the son of a Yetanti's son." (A lower case k and y will indicate these specific usages.)

If a male, or female, member of the Yetanti moiety is the grandchild of a male Keber, he, or she, is called "senkrayhura" (*hura* means child). A woman of the Keber moiety, a daughter of a male Keber, is called "senkra." A woman of the Yetanti moiety other than a senkrayhura is called "anazti" and is the granddaughter of a male Yetanti. Since descent is patrilineal, children belong to their father's moiety, but, as we have noted in the rules of marriage, their statuses do not reflect a simple, dual division. Children of a yetanti father and a senkra mother have the status of Yetanti in all matters except marriage, and are called "senkra-child" rather than "yetanti" or "anazti," as would be expected. A senkrayhura is regarded as a quasi-Keber in matters of marriage and cannot marry a Keber. This reflects the Keber prestige which is (or was) so great that it imparts a Keber quality even to a Keber's grandchildren.

The incest taboo, or marriage prohibitions, among the Qemant applies to all persons in one's moiety and once included all consanguineal (blood) relatives of the other moiety less than eight degrees removed from the person. During the past forty years, Qemant have gradually reduced the prohibition to relatives only four degrees removed from one, but they still speak of the old rule as proper.

DISTINCTIONS BETWEEN MOIETIES. As already mentioned, the positions of wambar and higher priest, the highest religious and political offices in Qemant society, are held by members of the Keber moiety. Spokesmen for the wambar and majordomos are also Kebers. Lower priests and guardians of the sacred beer are Yetantis.

Until recently, any keber elder had an established judicial role as an informal mediator and counselor. If a yetanti (or a senkrahura) had a grievance, he would go to a keber, kiss his knee, and state his problem. The keber elder would mediate the case, threatening ostracism or malediction by the priesthood as the potential punishment. The power accorded to the role of a keber elder is an indication of the near class difference between the Keber and the Yetanti moieties. However, the role of a keber elder today as an informal mediator is not different from the role of an elder who is a yetanti or senkrayhura.

No distinction exists today between the clothing, houses, and equipment of Kebers and Yetantis, and there is no apparent difference in wealth between them. Some people say that Kebers have or formerly had more land than Yetantis, but no evidence was found to support this statement. Until approximately thirty years ago, it was customary at ceremonies for Kebers to sit apart from Yetantis and in better seats. Kebers were served food and drink and were given water to wash their hands after all members of the priesthood had been thus served but before all Yetantis who were not priests. It is said that in the last century a young Keber could not pour a beverage or serve food to an older Yetanti, but an older Yetanti could serve a younger Keber. Today, when a Yetanti meets a Keber, he still bows and is expected to kiss the knee of the Keber, but he seldom does the latter.

In all, there is a classlike structure in Qemant society with the Yetanti moiety somewhat subordinate to the Keber moiety. There is also a third, distinctly lower, stratum, which consists of former hereditary slaves. These people are Negroids, whose homeland was the western lowlands of Ethiopia. Formerly slaves in the Qemant area, they now work as sharecroppers or as servants. A person who is half Negroid and half Qemant is called *mawalid* (mixed one). During the time of slavery, some Negro women were concubines or just random sexual partners. If, under these circumstances, a woman bore a child, the owner of the mother kept the child as a slave.

PATRICLANS. Oral genealogies of Kebers trace ancestors through an agnatic (related by males) line for approximately fourteen generations to one of nine culture heroes who are the founders of nine clearly defined clans (see Fig. 1). Yetantis trace their ancestry similarly except that the clans are not as clearly defined and there are no specific Yetanti culture heroes. Most Yetanti genealogies terminate in a Keber culture hero. Qemant say that the ancestors of the Keber are "pure" Qemant, whereas the ancestors of the Yetanti are Qemant who married with "other people," who are not identified.

Today, the Keber and Yetanti clans have no corporate functions (such as ownership of property) and only limited territoriality. For example, the Nazi,

Yengasi, and Yezana clans of the Keber moiety are dispersed throughout the eastern half of the Qemant area around Karkar (see Fig. 1 for other examples). Centuries ago, however, the Qemant clans probably had more clearly demarcated territories and stronger corporate aspects. Each of the ancestral culture heroes at the apex of every clan have one or more sacred groves dedicated to them. Sacrifice by Qemant in the groves is the last tenuous link between the now scattered members of each clan and their deified apical ancestor.

The ascending agnatic lines of the clans are never used in tracing ownership of land, but claims may be made through these lines for election to a politicoreligious position. In this case, a candidate will recount his genealogy in order to demonstrate the number of his ancestors who have held politicoreligious office. Any of the three clans of the Keber moiety in Karkar or of the three in Chelga could supply, respectively, candidates for the positions of wambar of Karkar and of Chelga. Certain clans of the two moieties supply candidates for the priesthood and for the minor politicoreligious positions discussed earlier. Each patriclan consists of many segments, or patrilineages,[2] and, for reasons that are no longer known to informants, members of the priesthood are drawn from certain of these lineages. At present, lineages have no other functions and are not designated by names.

The functional significance of unilineality as it exists today concerns principally rules of marriage and religious offices. Certain other customs also reflect unilineality. A child receives his father's first or main name as his last name, and personal qoles and zars may be inherited homolineally, through patrilineal lines for men or matrilineal lines for women.

Residence after marriage but before the newlywed couple builds a house is duolocal at first, the groom living with his parents and the bride with her parents. Residence then gradually becomes patrilocal or, at times, matrilocal, the married couple living with the groom's parents or with the bride's parents. (Customs of early residence are discussed in Chapter 9.) Residence after construction of a house is usually patrilocal; a son builds a house near that of his father after approximately three to five years of marriage. Small extended families are most common, but large extended families of two or more siblings or cousins and their children are also found. Strife in a man's family or certain economic circumstances may lead to ambilocality. The married couple according to personal preferences sets up residence near the wife's parents or other kin of the wife, or near kin of the husband other than his father. Ambilocality is common, and residence among the Qemant might be described as patrilocal in ideal, but in actual practice, it is often ambilocal. It may very well be that the Qemant were strictly patrilocal and patrilineal in former centuries, but have been gradually making a transition to ambilocality and ambilineality (this last term is defined in the following section). As discussed earlier, patrilineality is retained on the levels of moiety and clan in Qemant social organization, especially where it is integrated with their religion.

---

[2] The "patri-" signifies that the lineage or clan is organized along lines of patrilineal descent.

Ambilineal Organization and Land Tenure

Although descent is reckoned patrilineally among the Qemant in determining kin groups, to which certain societal roles are assigned, customs of mutual aid sometimes follow and customs of inheritance of property always follow ambilineal reckoning. Rights to the use of land are based upon kinship traced ambilineally, as in the following sentences which explain ambilineality. In justifying or establishing claims to use land, any of the sixteen great-great-grandparents may be used, and rights to land are usually traced to still more distant ancestors. Claims are made through a single line of descent traced generation after generation back and forth in any way from male to female ancestors, hence ambilineally, to the ancestor who first cultivated the land.

Because the Qemant are markedly patrilocal and ties of patrilineality are more binding than other ties of kinship, most aid that is required immediately or is of a minor scale comes from patrilineal relatives living nearby. Thus when aid is needed, Erada the plowman calls upon his sons, then upon his brothers and their sons, and finally upon some of the sons of his father's brothers. When much help is needed, kin of all kinds are recruited, and, if necessary, recruitment goes beyond kin to fellow members of associations, fictive kin, and unrelated neighbors. (Fictive kinship and associational bonds are examined later in this chapter.)

A person allows his ambilineal ties to wax and wane in strength according to his needs for labor and for support in claiming rights to use land. A Qemant may rely on local ambilineal kin to give assistance in projects requiring labor and when he is involved in a dispute. Ambilineal kin who live far away attend weddings, funerals, and other rites of passage, but may not be depended upon for labor. It is the duty of the ambilineal kin group to avenge a member's murder or to raise blood money that must be paid by a member of the group. A Qemant may be injured or murdered in revenge for an act committed by a member of his ambilineal descent group.

Strife and litigation arise over rights to use land if a claim is made to land being cultivated by others. Such claims most often lead to strife when a person "activates" an ambilineal line of descent that has long been dormant with respect to use rights of land. A Qemant never owns land, but holds it by usufruct (in this case, the right to enjoy the fruit of the land owned by one's kinship group) or else rents it from someone who holds use right. When a man dies, his wife retains half of their portable property, which is owned jointly, and the other half is divided equally among their children. However, the wife receives none of her husband's rights to use land, which can be claimed only through ties of consanguineal (blood) kinship. Nominally, sons and daughters inherit equal rights to the use of land that their father tilled and to the dormant or unactivated rights to other land, which may be claimed by their father's ambilineal kin.

A Qemant male rarely activates his wife's rights to land, however, for such action would lead to strife with his wife's kin. He usually leaves such rights to his wife's brothers. A husband may activate long dormant rights of his wife's family if the land is near plots that he is cultivating. For example, Erada cultivates a few small plots controlled by Adonech's ambilineal kin group.

Rest is the term Qemant give to the use rights to land that a person or a family claims or can potentially claim; hence "usufruct" in this sense. Rest also means "freehold" and is also used as the opposite of gult (roughly translated, fief). A secondary use of rest as usufruct refers to use rights in other communities which are nominally claimable but for which there is no hope of activating the rights. If a Qemant has few claims to usufruct, or if he wishes to consolidate his cultivated plots near his house, he may hold some plots as a tenant. In this case, he may in turn rent to another person his rights in outlying land. Rights of tenancy are not heritable.

In Karkar and in some parts of Chelga, Qemant pay land taxes (asrat or tithe of annual crops) on rest they use. Until a few years ago the taxes were collected by local Amhara feudal officials. Amhara officials of a low rank called farasanya (literally, horseman) still supervise collection of the tax, but it is now paid directly to a tax collector of the national Ministry of Finance. Farasanyas also collect a tax called chaw (bar of salt) for themselves. Asrat and chaw are now paid with Ethiopian currency, but until recently were rendered in grain, honey, and other produce, and in salt bars, which were a common medium of exchange. Today, each cultivator of land must also pay taxes for education and for health. The total of all types of taxes paid by residents of greater Karkar during 1965 was Eth. $6381.

The Qemant in other communities do not pay asrat, but pay higher taxes, called yamsho maret, to a feudal vassal (gult gaz or fief ruler). These taxes are levied upon gult lands. As a reward for prowess in battle and loyalty to a ruler, the feudal vassal is granted several rights over all or part of one or more communities. Among these are rights to collect taxes, hold judicial court, and levy corvee. Rights thus given to a ruler's military vassal are called gult. In Ethiopia, as in Europe during feudal times, there is a hierarchy of titles and roles among vassals:

Negusa Nagast	King of kings (emperor)
Negus	King
Ras	Head (duke)
Dajazmach	Commander of the reserves
Fitawrari	Commander of the vanguard
Kanyazmach	Commander of the right flank
Gerazmach	Commander of the left flank

Other titles, not in hierarchical order:

Balambaras	Keeper of fortified height
Shalaka	Leader of one thousand
Basha	Leader of troops with firearms
Leul	Title of royalty
Lej	Title of royalty and nobility
Bajerond	Treasurer
Azaz	Commander
Gaz	Local ruler

Farasanya	Horseman (comparable to German *Ritter* and French *chevalier*)
Shambal	(Captain)
Mato Alaka	Leader of one hundred
Amsa Alaka	Leader of fifty
Aser Alaka	Leader of ten
Cheqa Shum	(Sheriff)

These rights and the titles may or may not be inherited, and can be revoked for disloyalty or lack of strong support of a ruler. Subinfeudation is also found; that is, a vassal may in turn have his own vassals.

Karkar used to be a *gult*, but was removed from this status when the Qemant in Karkar became nominal Christians during the program of enforced baptism during the reign of Johannes IV. As the national government has become modernized since World War II, vassals have ceased to be appointed, although they are still common. Therefore, feudal taxes on *gult* are beginning to be eliminated in favor of asrat, taxes on *rest*, paid to the national government.

Qemant Kinship Terminology

The web of Qemant kinship embraces named social positions, and anthropologists have long studied and classified such names, or kinship terms, for several reasons. Through the study of these kinship terms and the interaction of kin, the ideal behavior of people can be compared with their actual behavior. For example, among the Qemant four different categories of male relatives in the parental generation (see Table 1) are called *ag*. All *ags* are ideally thought, and labeled or termed, to be socially equal. However in practice a man rarely traces claims to land by ambilineal, or other, links through mother's brother and never through mother's sister's husband, both of whom are referred to as *ag*. *Ags* who fill the social positions of father's brothers are behaviorally quite distinct from all other *ags*, as they are the relatives a man turns to for everyday aid, which, we have already noted, is claimed patrilineally. Comparative studies of kinship terminology are additionally useful in tracing, or disproving, historical connections between two or more peoples. Anthropologists also study kinship terms in order to explore semantics and human perception.

In Lewis Henry Morgan's pioneering scheme of classification, developed in the nineteenth century, the system of the Qemant is descriptive; that is, no collateral kin are merged terminologically with lineal kin. (Collaterals are blood relations not directly connected by descent with one's previous generation.) According to the widely used Spier-Murdock classification, based principally upon terms for cousins, kin terms of the Qemant are of the Eskimo type. The Yankees also have the Eskimo system in which terms for siblings are distinct from terms for cousins. In the classification proposed by Robert H. Lowie, depending principally upon the patterns of terms in the parental generation, the terminological system is lineal. This means that collaterals, such as mother's brother and father's

TABLE 1.
QEMANT KINSHIP TERMINOLOGY AND PATRIMOIETY MEMBERSHIP [a]

Relative [b]	Qemant term (Falasha term)	Amhara term	Patrimoiety membership ego's	opposite
FaFa	An	Emita	X	
FaMo	Tan	Emita		X
MoFa	An	Emita		X
MoMo	Tan	Emita	X	
Fa	Aba	Abat	X	
Mo	Gana	Enat		X
FaBr, FaSi	Ag, ter	Agot, akest	X	
MoBr, MoSi	Ag, ter	Agot, akest		X
FaBrWi, FaSiHu	Ter, ag	Yagotbal, yakestbal		X
MoBrWi, MoSiHu	Ter, ag	Yagotbal, yakestbal	X	
WiFa	Anshen	Amat		X
WiMo	Tanshen	Amat	X	
BrSi	Zan, shan	Wandem, ehet	X	
Wi	Wina	Mist		X
FaBrSo, FaBrDa	Aghura	Yagotlej	X	
FaSiSo, FaSiDa	Terhura	Yakestlej		X
MoBrSo, MoBrDa	Aghura	Yagotlej		X
MoSiSo, MoSiDa	Terhura	Yakestlej	X	
WiBr, WiSi	Anshen, warsa	Amach, warsa		X
BrWi, SiHu	Warsa, anshen	Warsa, amach		X
WiBrWi, WiSiHu	Warsa, anshen	Agabuny	X	
So, Da	Hura	Lej	X	
BrSo, BrDa	Zanahura	Yawandemlej	X	
SiSo, SiDa	Shanahura	Yahetlej		X
SoWi, DaHu	Sergu, anshen	Merat, amach		X
WiBrSo, WiBrDa	Anshenhura	Yamachlej		X
WiSiSo, WiSiDa	Warsayhura	Yawarsalej	X	
SoSo, SoDa	Hurayhera	Yalejlej	X	
DaSo, DaDa	Hurayhera	Yalejlej		X
Hu (w.s.)	Gerwa	Bal		

[a] *Note:* Qemant and Falasha kin terms are always prefixed by the pronoun marker *ye-* (my). The *ya-/y-* prefix in the Amhara terms means "of-."

[b] Fa, father; Mo, mother; Br, brother; Si, sister; Hu, husband; Wi, wife; So, son; Da, daughter; w.s., wife speaking.

brother, are terminologically distinct from lineal kin (from father, for example), but not from one another.[3]

It should be noted that the kinship terminology of the Cushitic-speaking Qemant has nearly the same pattern as that of the Semitic-speaking Amhara, but the terms themselves are almost entirely different. Falasha who still speak the Agaw language use the same terms as the Qemant, with slight differences in pronunciation. Falasha who speak Amharic use only the Amhara terms of kinship.

---

[3] Students will find Ernest L. Schusky's *Manual for Kinship Analysis* (New York, Holt, Rinehart and Winston, Inc., 1965) helpful in understanding the discussion in this chapter, and they might find Table 1 useful as a source of kinship terms to be used in conjunction with the explanations and exercises in the *Manual*.

No matter what the term of kinship may be for each relative, a Qemant is always conscious of the fact that his kinsmen belong to one or the other of the two moieties. Reflection on this fact may come at the time of marriage, in a discussion of positions in the priesthood, or at other times. The cognitive map a Qemant has of his society is of two distinct but interrelated social structures, those of the Keber and the Yetanti. Formation of this dual cognitive map (see Table 1) begins with a child's first awareness that if father is a Keber, then mother must be a Yetanti.

Fictive Kinship

FICTIVE PARENT-CHILD RELATIONSHIPS. Among the pagan-Hebraic Qemant an old custom of fictive parent-child relationships called *engohura* (breast child) exists, but is less common than Christian godparenthood among Christian Qemant. People who think they need the bonds of fictive kinship enter into such relationships as fictive children. This relationship is especially sought if a person does not have many affinal and consanguineal relatives (related by marriage and by blood), or if he lacks land and other wealth. Wealthier people become fictive parents in order to gain supporters and labor and, after they are dead, mourners.

An adult wishing to become a fictive child finds an older couple, usually of at least average wealth, as his fictive parents; if the person is a child, the couple is selected for him. This was the case when Zawdu, six years of age, was adopted by Ayo, the shaman, and his wife, who have four daughters but no sons. On a pleasant, cool day early in the dry season, the fictive parent-child relationship was initiated with a minor ceremony in which Ayo and his wife coated their thumbs with honey; the thumbs are said to symbolize the nipples of a woman's breast. Little Zawdu then sucked their thumbs to symbolize his dependency on the couple, who then vowed to act as parents toward their fictive child. Ayo and his wife are now called *engoaba* (breast father) and *engogana* (breast mother) by their fictive child, and they call him *engohura* (breast child), a name which is also applied to the entire complex of relationships. Throughout and beyond life, a reciprocal parent-child relationship exists between Zawdu, the breast child, and his fictive parents.

If the breast child has not yet married, the breast parents find a suitable spouse and provide, for a girl, the dowry and the wedding feast and, for a boy, the bride price. If the breast child has no "true" parents or if the true parents are very poor, he or she lives with and works for the breast parents and inherits use rights to land and property from them just like a natural child. Even if the breast child does not reside with the breast parents, the relationship is close. When a breast parent dies, the breast child provides a funeral, and later conducts an annual ceremony of prayer, and provides the *tazkar* ceremony. This rite is necessary in Qemant religion for admission of the deceased to heaven; thus the breast child reciprocates by conducting a very important ritual.

Breast parenthood is known but rare among the Amhara of Bagemder. Christian godparenthood, called *abalej* (father-child) is practiced by most Amhara and is very common among the Christian Qemant. On a child's day of baptism his *yakrestenabat* and *yakrestenaenat* (godfather and godmother) vow to treat the child as their own. However, this assurance is not as strong as the vow of breast parenthood, and the institution of godparenthood is less binding than breast parenthood.

FICTIVE SIBLINGS. Another form of fictive kinship, called *mize*, exists among the Qemant. *Mize* means a fictive brother or sister and also means a whole group of fictive siblings. The nucleus of one's mize-group is formed when one marries (see discussion of marriage in Chapter 9). Mize-groups are primarily monosexual, for males or for females, but those for women are of minor importance. The exception to monosexuality of mize-groups is that a man's mize-brothers pledge a fictive, brother-sister relationship to his bride before the marriage ceremony. After a man is married, members are added and dropped from his mize-group, but new members do not pledge a fictive bond of kinship with the wife. Members of one's mize-group must be at least seven degrees removed from oneself in consanguineal kinship.

Every person has his own mize-group; thus, all of the mize-siblings in the group are not necessarily fictive siblings of one another. The only relationship they have in common is the fictive siblinghood with the central person in the mize-group. This mize-group is defined in relation to a given person, and all of the fictive siblings of a given person do not usually meet with him at any one time. Certain mizes of one person might, however, also be mizes of others, and might also be members of a person's *mahebar*, a voluntary association discussed later.

The incest taboo applied to consanguineal kin is extended to fictive kin of the mize. (This extension of the incest taboo is not found in the institution of mize among the Amhara of Bagemder, who also have mize-groups.) Hence, the children of two mize cannot marry one another or one another's consanguineal kin who are not at least seven degrees removed. Also, a person cannot marry any of his mizes' consanguineal kin who are not at least seven degrees removed from the mize. Of late, these rules have been reduced to three or four degrees in actual practice.

The obligations and responsibilities of two persons in a mize relationship approximate those between siblings. They exchange labor, give reciprocal aid during strife, contribute reciprocally to feasts at the various rites of passage, and give reciprocal aid in other ways when it is needed.

BOND FRIENDSHIP. Ordinary friends are called *mahala*, and the same term is used for a special or "bond" friendship in which the participants give reciprocal services and discuss problems and matters not discussed with others. Bond friends give one another special names, used only by themselves and only within the context of the bond friendship. Such bond friendship is often, but not always, reinforced by ties of kinship, fictive kinship, or common membership in an association.

Associational Ties

An association, sometimes called a nonkinship group, is the social structure within which most of the activities of industrial societies, with their atrophied kinship networks, are performed. For example an average Yankee may work for an industrial corporation, belong to a labor union, attend a church, and relax with others in a bowling league, while being protected by still other associations of police, fire fighters, and health workers. Associations are additionally found in peasant societies like that of the Qemant. In any society, the complexity and maximum size of kinship groups are limited, and their membership is ascribed rather than achieved (social position assigned, as by birth, instead of attained, as by volition). Most societies circumvent the limitations of kinship groups with associational groups, often classified according to the manner of recruitment of members into the group. For example, the Cushitic-speaking Galla, distant neighbors of the Qemant, have a society founded upon *gada* associations, a system of age groupings each of which contains members whose ages span eight years and each ranked in a hierarchy: boys, herders, warriors, leaders, and elders. Other associations of other peoples are based upon the two sexes; so-called men's clubs, women's clubs, and secret societies found among many primitive peoples are examples.

Associations founded upon agreement or contract, usually oral, are very common among peoples of the world, and particularly among the Qemant. Contractual associations have a voluntary, sometimes ceremonial, initiation of members, but in some instances once the contract is made the new member of the association may not leave. Among the Qemant, a person may leave an association by his own free will, but thereby runs the risk of being friendless. Apropos of this, members of one mutual-aid association still mutter over their beer about "that bastard Ayo." It seems he withdrew from the association and reneged upon his obligation to render aid after he himself had earlier received aid from the group. In still other instances, some Qemant have been unceremoniously ejected from an association.

ASSOCIATION AND ASSOCIATES. The *mahebar* ("association") is a voluntary association found among the Qemant and Amhara. Ideally, the group has at least twelve members, but it often has more. A fellow member of the mahebar is called a *mahebaranya* ("associate"), and members are often bound to each other by additional ties of kinship, fictive kinship, or bond friendship. Separate associations exist for men and for women, but some spouses of either sex may participate in the minor feast which each association holds monthly. Associations for men are far more important than those for women.

A group of men of approximately the same age form an association whose membership may change through time. Membership provides pleasurable fellowship, centering upon shared food and drink, labor for construction and agriculture, aid when one is involved in a dispute, and individual guarantors when needed in litigation. The members also form a pool to lend oxen, tools, seed grain, and money to one another. They contribute food and labor for members' rites of passage, particularly the rite for admission to heaven. Reciprocity is the keynote of membership. It a member does not "balance his account" with other members of the association over a period of time, he is warned first and then eventually expelled from the group.

The women's mahebar is formed in the same way as the men's, but it does not have economic or judicial functions and reciprocal labor is never expected. Goals of the women's mahebar are principally expressive. Meetings are held during the day at various times during the month, at which the women usually spin, sew, and gossip.

On the Thursday of each month dedicated to Mezgana and on the Thursday dedicated to Gebarhu, the Qemant hold their largest and most important mahebars. These meetings are held only in communities where there are still people of the pagan-Hebraic faith. These associations, which were mentioned earlier in discussing the council of elders, had large memberships of thirty or more men until the 1950s, but the numbers are now diminished. Meetings of the formal council of elders are held early during the gathering of the associations on Mezgana's day. Members of this major association may also belong to one or more minor associations that hold meetings at fixed times to honor pagan-Hebraic culture heroes or holy beings who have local importance. Among the Christian Qemant, the mahebar meets one or two Sundays a month and, as we have noted, bears an additional name, *sanbate* (Sunday association).

8

The Annual Round of Economic and Religious Endeavor

THE CROPS AND ANIMALS of a Qemant peasant are used not only for his family's subsistence but also to pay taxes levied by the secular officials, to support religious organizations and community and familial festivities and ceremonies, to exchange for needed and desired goods and services produced by others, and most important to provide seed and stock for future production of more crops and animals.

In food production, the peasant uses both empirical technology and supernatural practice to wrest a yield from the land. Supernaturalism regulates the annual round of economic endeavor and is integrated with specific aspects of this endeavor, but Qemant do not confuse empirical cause and effect with that of the supernatural. For example, as a form of insurance against unforeseen, generalized disaster which might befall the crops and the community, sowing does not begin until the wambar conducts the annual rites of fertility. To insure the proper amount of rain for the crops, rain-regulating ceremonies are held to increase or to decrease rainfall. However, Qemant do not believe supernaturalism takes the place of backbreaking plowing, vigorous weeding, bone-chilling irrigation, and tedious mending of fences at the correct time and with skillful technique.

Since Qemant technology and other empirical knowledge are not always sufficient to control the capricious occurrences in nature, supernaturalism is used to effect Qemant adaptation to the environment. Therefore, a fence and a boy armed with a stick protect a field from an errant flock of sheep, but a prayer protects the same field from a chance invasion of locusts or a grass fire.

Production in the Qemant Economy

The economy of the Qemant is based principally upon cultivation of edible plants. Agriculture is a full-time occupation for all Qemant except the wambar, who is a full-time politicoreligious specialist, and the priests and local feudal officials, who are only part-time cultivators.

TILLING THE SOIL. Like other Qemant men, Erada and his sons prepare the fields for planting, using a wooden scratch plow, with an iron-shod tip, which is pulled by two oxen. Beginning sometime in or after February, they plow the soil three or four times in several directions, to a depth of about 8 inches, seldom removing stones from the rocky soil. Furrows cannot be seen, as the entire surface of a field is completely turned over.

All crops, with the exception of a variety of barley, are sown once a year during the major rainy season from June through September (see Fig. 3). The men and boys, sometimes aided by women and girls, sow grains, pulses, and oil seeds by the broadcast method and plant potatoes, cucurbits, garlic, and shallots in the ground by hand. Fields are replowed to cover the seeds. No attempt is made to select seeds that will produce superior crops. Crops are rotated when fields begin to lose their fertility, but little fallowing is done.

All males and females in Erada's family weed fields with an iron-bladed hoe or with their hands. Erada usually does not fertilize his fields, as animal dung is a major source of fuel in the Qemant region. Erada and his neighbors depend upon rain to water their fields and seldom irrigate them artificially. An exception is made for the most important crop, the cereal *tef*, which needs a very wet soil to germinate. If rain does not make the ground wet enough to sow tef, irrigation channels are made with a plow to lead water into the tef fields. Occasionally, small gardens of shallots, garlic, and cayenne pepper are irrigated by this method for out-of-season yields. When necessary, fields are also drained by plowed channels.

A Qemant's fields are separated from his neighbor's by low walls of stones and fences of acacia branches. Low earthen ridges, a plowed furrow, or several piles of stones placed at intervals are also used as dividers. The acacia fences are also used to keep animals out of the fields when crops are growing.

Harvesting of cereals, oil seeds, and pulses is usually done by males, but females help when needed. Squatting on the ground, the reaper bunches the stalks with one hand and draws an iron sickle with a smooth, knifelike cutting edge across them with the other. Threshing is done by males on a circular threshing floor 9 to 12 feet in diameter, which is ringed with stones and plastered with a mixture of mud and dung. A wooden pitchfork is used to throw the sun-dried grain or legumes onto the floor, where two or more oxen, with mouths tied shut to prevent them from eating, are driven around to trample the grain. Stacks of the oil seed *nug* and of mustard seed are threshed by flailing them with a stout wooden stick. Grain is winnowed with a wooden shovel, pitchfork, or flat basket used as a grain scoop. Finally, the winnowed grain is put into bags of hide, strapped onto donkeys, and taken home for storage in granaries.

Older Qemant techniques of horticulture are still retained in certain instances. Land in a few areas too steep for plowing is cleared by slashing the brush and trees and then burning them to complete the clearing of the field and to reduce them to ashes which fertilize the plot. Cultivation is done with an iron-bladed hoe. (The hoe is the typical implement of horticultural tillage, just as the plow is the tool of agricultural tillage.) Garden plots (*wajad*) near houses are also cultivated by men and women using the hoe. These gardens usually provide all plants used for food by the Qemant besides the all-important grains, legumes, and oil seeds raised in the larger fields.

TENDING THE LIVESTOCK. Animal husbandry is much less important than plant cultivation. A variety of zebu cattle is the most important kind of livestock and is used for meat and milk. Oxen of these cattle are used for plowing. Milking is usually done by males, but may be done by females. Milk, butter, and curds are the dairy products consumed. Sheep and goats are second in importance to cattle, and are used for meat, wool, and hides, but are rarely milked. In accord with Hebraic dietary laws, the Qemant cannot eat pork or the flesh of any animal that has been bitten, and thus polluted, by a hyena. Donkeys and a smaller number of mules and horses are used only as beasts of burden and for riding; their hides are not used. Dogs are used to guard homes, cats are kept to protect grain from vermin, and every household has several chickens. Almost every family has several long, cylindrical beehives made of woven wattles. The hives produce a moderate supply of honey.

HUNTING AND GATHERING. Game is scarce and hunting is unimportant. Fish are abundant, but eating them is tabooed. A very few wild foods are gathered, including certain wild fruits and spices. Wild plant materials for crafts and household uses are still important and include straw for basketry, wild fruits used in making soap, and other plants used for dyes and medicine.

The land in part of Wali Dava is too steep for the use of the plow and oxen; thus slash-and-burn horticulture with hoes is used for crop production.

PRODUCING CRAFTS. Like the Amhara, the Qemant disdain manual labor other than in agricultural pursuits. Only four occupational roles are practiced and held in esteem by the Qemant and Amhara, those of agriculturalist, soldier, political leader, and priest. In fact, the Qemant and Amhara have such a general disdain for work done with the hands that when the subject is broached, they quote a proverb: "It is better to marry a man who speaks eloquently than to marry a man who works with his hands."

No Qemant craftsmen produce goods for the market, but domestic crafts of several kinds are well developed. Women make baskets, using a coil technique, and, in the lowlands they also make mats of a checked pattern. Men make rope and twine of grass and animal hair, and they make querns and pestles of stone. Thatching of roofs and carpentry in constructing houses, furniture, and plows are also done by men. If a man is especially skilled in carpentry, he may do such work for a neighbor in return for goods or labor in his fields. Iron tools and pottery are obtained for goods or money from Falasha smiths, who are male, and potters, who are female. A Qemant woman spins her own cotton on a spindle whorl, twirling it in her hand. The thread thus spun is taken to a male Falasha or Muslim weaver, who produces cloth from it. Leather goods are acquired from a special occupational group of tanners, called *Arabenya*, who are endogamous and speak Amharic, but who are not considered by others as Amhara.

Distribution in the Qemant Economy

The Qemant have at least four modes of distributing their production. Allocation of goods and services may be by formal market exchange inside of a marketplace, by informal market exchange outside of a marketplace, by collection and redistribution in connection with ritual, and by reciprocity. A large part of Qemant exchange is not transacted within their interesting, busy marketplaces and, as we shall see, their market places bustle with activities other than trade.

FORMAL MARKETING. Means of transportation and communication in the Qemant region are poorly developed, and the Qemant peasant has access only to his own regional marketing system, which is little affected by conditions outside Qemant society. Marketing, formal and informal, is the exchange of goods and services at prices arrived at by supply and demand.

Money is almost always used in formal marketing and is sometimes employed in informal marketing. Today the official Ethiopian copper and paper currency is used as the principal medium of exchange. Although they are not official currency of the nation, silver Maria Theresa coins, minted in Austria during the late 1700s and thereafter, are still used, and some people hoard them because of their silver content. Salt bars, an ancient medium of exchange that was replaced by modern coinage about fifty years ago, might still be regarded as a minor medium of exchange since they are conventionally used to reward priests for certain of their services.

Formal marketing is held at fixed times in marketplaces, usually little

Typical Saturday market in Gondar. The wild fig tree in the center of the market place is about 300 years old and was planted around the time (early 1600s) of the building of the castle, on the horizon at the right, by the Emperor Fasil, who founded Gondar inside of Qemantland.

more than vacant clearings when the market is not being held. Until a decade ago, markets were held once a week in uncultivated areas of Qemant communities and sometimes in or near administrative villages of the Amhara, and were part of a regional weekly cycle of markets that covered six days of the week. Two former marketplaces in Karkar are still called Monday market (Sanyogabaya) and Friday market (Arbgabaya). A Wednesday market (Robit) is still operated in Chela, on the southwestern edge of Karkar. The Saturday market is still held in nearby Gondar Town. Today, administrative and market villages, such as Aykel, Saraba, and Tekel Denga, in which a minor market is held six days a week and a major market once or twice a week, have replaced older marketplaces in many parts of the Qemant area. There are additional new administrative and market villages just outside of the Qemant area which the Qemant use. The most important marketplace for Bagemder and Semen has existed since about 1600 and is in the town of Gondar which now has a daily market in addition to the older, major market on Saturday.

For the Qemant peasant, trading at a marketplace is a means of exchanging a commodity of which he has a slight surplus for another commodity which he lacks. Occasionally, services are performed, as when tanners in the marketplace cover storage baskets with leather. Commodities that the Qemant need include some otherwise unobtainable plant products, such as cotton from the lowlands; mineral products available only in distant areas, such as salt from the Danakil Depression; and products, such as Falasha iron ware, of local crafts in which the Qemant do not engage. Machinemade goods, originating abroad or in Ethiopian cities, are rare in the markets except those in towns and villages on the main provincial road. Traders in town markets, such as Gondar, Azazo, and Gorgora, and in village markets include Ethiopian and Arab full-time middlemen and some peasants selling a part of their surplus. In marketplaces in the countryside, the few full-time traders are usually itinerants, and local peasants do most of the selling.

TO MARKET, TO MARKET, TO HEAR THE LATE NEWS. The marketplace functions for the Qemant in other ways besides exchange. Most important, it provides a sort of social glue for the Qemant. Married women, who live among their husbands' kin, are reunited and may gossip with their siblings and former neighbors during not-so-chance meetings in the marketplace. Relatives and friends have a legitimate excuse, buying or selling, to take a day off from labor in the home or fields and to catch upon the latest happenings to one another. A vendor may not sell all of her produce, but no matter, for going to market is always exhilarating, even without sales or purchases. In general, the centers of trade are homogenizers of ideas and modes of behavior, for one perceives here how members of local and distant communities are acting and thinking. In short, the marketplace greatly increases, on a regular basis, the number of face-to-face contacts a peasant can maintain.

In the marketplace, one might additionally see or learn of strangers in the community and hear the latest of the customary pronouncements from the local feudal officials. These officials have long guaranteed the peaceful existence of the marketplace so that their region will prosper, and produce taxes, through trade and commercial traffic to centers of trade. Through control and surveillance of markets, local officials can feel the pulse of their territory and stay attuned to the moods of the populace.

INFORMAL MARKETING. Informal marketing consists of exchange between two persons in which middlemen are not involved, and money is seldom used. This trade may be transacted anywhere in a community at almost any time. In most transactions, a certain amount of one commodity is deemed equal in value to a certain amount of another commodity and the two are exchanged. Before livestock is exchanged, however, the price of the beasts is agreed upon in Maria Theresa dollars. If one of the parties in the transaction receives an animal worth less than the one he has given, he receives additional produce priced at the number of Maria Theresas needed to balance the exchange.

COLLECTION AND REDISTRIBUTION. The third mode of distribution ties in with Qemant religious practices and kinship, and consists of collection and redistribution, in connection with ceremonies, of beverages and raw and processed foods. Peasants contribute animals and food used by the wambar and the priests for sacrifices and feasts. Contributions are made according to a person's means, the wealthy donating more than the poor. However, at ceremonies every participant consumes to his capacity or until the supply is exhausted. At certain times in the year, everyone in a community is thus guaranteed a feast that includes meat, which is not ordinarily part of a poor person's diet. Collection and redistribution of food for use in rituals is sometimes based on kinship and membership in associations. For rites of passage, food is collected from people who are related to the persons undergoing the rites, and distributed among the members of the community. Distribution of food among the members of a community in connection with religious events provides bonds of solidarity and thus helps to maintain Qemant societal boundaries.

RECIPROCITY. Qemant distribute a significant part of their goods and services through modes of reciprocity. It may be a bond of reciprocity between breast father and breast child, between a man and his fictive mize brothers, among all members of a community mahebar association, or simply between two neighbors, interacting in a very limited context, who help one another with house repairs.

The items involved in reciprocal exchange are not easily equated. For example, a priest may use his influence on behalf of and give special blessings to a peasant who regularly feeds and occasionally labors for the priest. Two families might engage in a continuous round of giving gifts, including meals, to one another. A rich man may build up his social credit in the community by feeding and entertaining people and by giving rather generous compensation to those who occasionally till his fields for him.

Days of Labor and Days of Rest

DAILY ENDEAVOR AND DAILY BREAD. All days are workdays for the Qemant except the Sabbath and the days of Mezgana and Gebarhu, described later. For Erada and his family, a workday begins before dawn. After arising, Adonech stirs the fire and adds fresh fuel. A new fire may be made with a wooden fire drill, using pulverized dung for tinder. However, fires are almost never allowed to go out, and if she cannot find an ember among the ashes, Adonech sends one of her grandchildren to fetch a glowing coal from a neighbor's hearth. Adonech and her daughters-in-law, Sahay and Almaz, then prepare the first of the two meals of the day and consume it with their husbands and any other adults present. If the women intend to work in the fields, they must arise around 3:00 A.M. in order to accomplish necessary work in the house before going to the fields. If the women are not laboring in the fields, their work includes gathering wood and brush for the fire and hauling water from nearby streams or springs in large, heavy pots or in gourds. Water is not commonly drunk, but is used in washing and cooking, and is consumed in the form of beer (selah). Other tasks of the women include cleaning the house, caring for young children, gardening, handicrafts, and grinding grain.

After arising, Erada usually feeds his oxen, especially in the rainy season when the beasts cannot get their own fodder. As Erada steps out of his house, he feels the chill dampness of the dawn air, which by now is filled with the aroma of eucalyptus branches burning in the hearth. He also hears the livestock grunting and stirring and a rooster crowing. Erada and his three sons then eat the morning meal and leave for the day's work, which may include laboring in the fields, constructing a house, or marketing. If a man is an elder, like Erada, he may attend a judicial meeting.

The children, who usually eat after the adults, begin most of their chores after breakfast. The boys go into the pastures with the livestock. Qemant girls and very young boys stay at home and help their mothers with work.

The most important of Adonech's activities is the preparation of food, a task filling a large part of her day. Cooking and baking are done over the wood fire in a hearth of three stones. Meat is eaten only once every two weeks or less, so most meals and food consumed between meals consist of grains and legumes parched on an iron griddle or boiled in a shallow pot. A thick, tangy, heavy bread, made from spices and a coarse flour of various grains, is also eaten. The bread is slowly baked in a pottery oven or on a covered griddle made of pottery. Erada and his family demonstrate that Qemant cannot live by bread alone, as much grain is also consumed in the form of beer, brewed from various cereals, but mainly from barley. Leaves of a plant similar to hops, called *gasho*, are used for flavoring the beer. Coffee, which is very expensive and used only for special occasions, is well liked today but was formerly a forbidden food among Qemant. It is consumed with salt, or occasionally with honey. Milk is also consumed, especially by children.

One of the family's two daily meals usually consists of a zestful thick stew (*saweh*), and sour, circular, flat bread (*arah*) about one-half an inch thick and 2 feet in diameter. The stew, made with varieties of cayenne pepper and various other ingredients, including spices, butter, oil seeds, legumes, onions, and sometimes meat, is simmered for hours over the fire in a pottery vessel. The flat bread is baked on the pottery griddle with a mud cover in a few minutes and, when ready, is firm but porous. It is often made of tef, but may also be made of barley, wheat, sorghums, or maize. Food is served on the surface of a pedestaled basket, used as a table. Several of the breads are stacked on the basket and the steaming and fragrant stew is poured on them with care so that none spills over the edges. Pieces of the bread are then torn from the stack underlying the stew and used to pluck savory morsels from the stew or to dip into it. A soft cheese is sometimes added to the stew and is sometimes eaten alone with the bread.

At dusk Erada and his sons return from their labor, and his grandsons return with the flocks. After the cows have been milked, the second meal of the day is consumed. Later, the adults sit around the embers of the fire, drink beer, and talk over the events of the day; visitors may join in. Finally, the household becomes quiet as Erada and his family go to bed, and his two married sons retire to their respective houses. A man and his wife sleep together, sometimes with younger children.

REMEMBERING THE SABBATH AND THE DAYS OF MEZGANA AND GEBARHU. The Qemant do not hold religious ceremonies on the Sabbath, which is from dusk on Friday until dusk on Saturday. However, they are supposed to observe the day by complete rest, refraining from labor in the fields and all household chores. Pagan-Hebraic Qemant only partially adhere to their Sabbath rules; they do not perform heavy work, but they do carry out light tasks. In fact, I observed no less a person than the wambar's wife grinding grain on the Sabbath.

Although not usually observed as a day of rest, the Sabbath is respected as a holy day by most peoples of northern and central Ethiopia. The Qemant are set apart from their neighbors because in addition to observing the Sabbath as a day of rest, they also regularly observe other religious days of rest monthly. One Thursday of each month is the holiday of Mezgana (God); another Thursday is the holiday of Gebarhu, now an angel but perhaps a former minor deity. Both are observed in a manner similar to that of the Sabbath. No ceremonies are held in sacred groves, but Qemant pray and give food and drink to neighbors in the name of Mezgana or Gebarhu and hold meetings of their associations (*mahebars*). It is probable that two or more Thursdays per month were religious days of rest among the Qemant before the Hebraic Sabbath was added to their religion.

Qemant observe one or more additional days of rest each month on the holidays of the holy culture heroes associated with local sacred groves. One holiday is observed each month for each culture hero, and the number of days of rest thus depends upon the number of culture heroes and groves in each community. Some communities have only one grove; others have more. One of these monthly holidays of each year is more important than the others, and a ceremony is then held in the grove of the culture hero. On other holidays for the culture heroes, people rest but no ceremonies are conducted.

The Annual Cycle of Work and Religious Events

Economic and religious activities of the Qemant are interdependent, as the examination of their ceremonial calendar will show. All Ethiopian peasants and tribal peoples use supernaturalism to supplement their technological control of the environment, but the distinctive elements of Qemant religion set them apart from their neighbors and bind them internally. The fact that the ceremonies are held in groves of trees also makes the rites, and the Qemant performers of them, distinctive in the eyes of other peoples of northern and central Ethiopia, who say the Qemant "originated in wood [timber]" and "hold secret rites in groves of trees."

THE CALENDAR. The Qemant words for month and for moon are the same (*arfa*), which suggests that they once had a lunar calendar. Qemant give some notice to the annual procession of the stars across the skies and the phases of the moon. They have only a few names for astronomical bodies, however, and their modern calendar does not use any of these names or any indigenous knowledge of astronomy. Instead, they now use the calendar of Christian Ethiopia, which has twelve months of thirty days and one "month" of five or six days (see Fig. 3). This calendar lays almost seven years behind the Gregorian calendar; thus, September 11, 1965, marked the beginning of the Ethiopian year of 1958. Since the Qemant borrowed the calendar from the Amhara, they use the Amharic names for the months. Names of the seasons and of the days are, however, Qemantinya words. Like the Amhara and various peoples of the Middle East, the

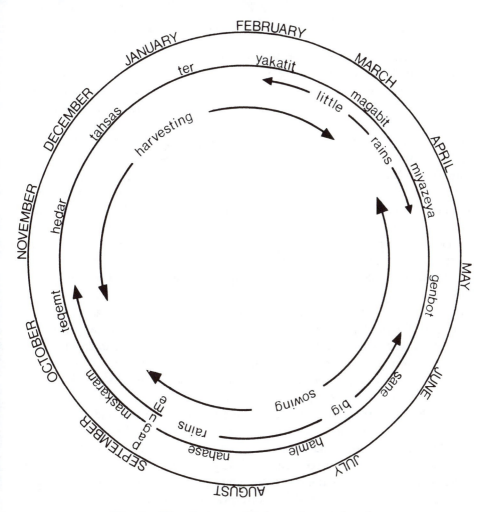

Fig. 3. The Qemant calendar and annual cycle.

Qemant reckon that the first hour of the day begins at dawn and that the twelfth hour ends at dusk. A second twelve-hour series follows until dawn. Since Qemant-land is near the equator, the time of sunset and sunrise does not vary much during the year. Hence, one o'clock in the morning, or dawn, occurs every day at almost the same point in the twenty-four hour cycle. During the daylight hours, approximate time is figured by the position of the sun, and Erada constantly amazed me with his reasonably accurate determinations of the hour.

THE START OF THE CEREMONIAL YEAR. The first month of the Ethiopian Christian calendar, *Maskaram*, begins on September 11, but the annual religious cycle of the Qemant does not begin until the second month, *Teqemt*. For this reason, we begin our account of the annual cycle in Qemantland with *Teqemt*, a time of early harvesting. On a Tuesday in *Teqemt*, the Qemant celebrate "the opening holiday" (*Balabeza*) of the sacred groves and the ceremonial year. This ceremony is held at Gelamezgana grove in Karkar which, as the name implies, is dedicated to Mezgana. A similar holiday is held in this grove on a Tuesday, later in the year, during the tenth month, *Hamle*. This holiday (*Balaleme*) closes all the groves and the ceremonial year until the season of heavy rains has passed. Gelamezgana is the only Qemant grove that has two ceremonies a year.

The opening and closing ceremonies used to be very important events which included the sacrificial offering of several sheep. Until a few years ago, no ceremony could be held in any grove until the regular ceremony of the opening holiday had been conducted by Qemant priests in Karkar. This ceremony reminded all Qemant from all communities of their dependence upon the great wambar of Karkar. Today, the opening and closing ceremonies are held by certain Christian Qemant in the community of Karkar, the last of whose pagan-Hebraic inhabitants were converted to Christianity within the past few years. Qemant priests in other communities now begin conducting other events of the annual cycle just as if the opening rite had been properly performed by fellow priests. A few ceremonies which are not held in groves may be held at any time.

Among pagan-Hebraic Qemant any ceremony conducted in the groves, other than a simple prayer session, is composed of the following major events. In preparation for a ceremony, members of the priesthood chew *koso*, a strong purge, for the three preceding days. On the eve of the ceremony the priests, and all laymen who will enter the grove, must abstain from sexual intercourse. The priests complete their rite of purification by washing themselves and their clothing. A fast is maintained by priests and laymen from the eve of the ceremony until after the sacrifice in the ceremony, on the next day.

On the morning of a ceremony, while the air is still cool and moist, music fills the air; a lower priest enters the grove playing a lyre, while a higher priest sprinkles honey, or milk and honey, on the sacred ground and trees. If a wambar is present, he leads the procession into the grove and sits down at the center; others must stand. At this time, a steady tramp of feet may be heard as all pagan-Hebraic Qemant enter the dense grove of varied trees, which often teems with birds and sometimes with monkeys. Christian Qemant participating in the ceremony must wait quietly outside the grove. The two priests then chant and pray for about an hour to the holy culture hero for whom the grove is named. Once again, members of a Qemant community reaffirm their bond with one of their ancestors, and through him, with one another. The priests, and, if he is present, the wambar then move to the outer edge of the verdant grove, usually heavily scented with aromatic gum oozing from the flat-topped acacia trees. Again, the lower priest plucks his lyre and the higher priest sprinkles honey on the ground and trees. Finally, the crowd is blessed and is allowed to sit down, but Christians must take seats apart from Qemant of the "old religion." The priests sit aloofly apart from all laymen.

Prayers, chants, and blessings are recited almost entirely in Qemantinya, but some Geez words are also used. (Geez, the ancient Ethiopic language, is still used today by the Ethiopian Orthodox Church.) Qemant claim that they do not understand all the Qemantinya words used in the ceremony because they are archaic and no longer used in everyday speech.

The next phase of the ceremony consists of the important sacrificial offering of blood, followed by a feast. Animals intended for sacrifice move about as they unknowingly await their part in the ceremony. These beasts are

Priests and elders finish butchering the animals.

provided by people in the community where the grove is located. At very large ceremonies there are usually several pairs of priests and many animals for sacrifice, and a large crowd gathers. Some sacred groves, such as those of Keberwa and Kadasti, contain a sacrificial altar which may be a single, large stone or a pile of small stones. In most groves and at other sacred sites, however, animals are slaughtered on the ground. The lower priest holds the legs of the animal while the higher priest cuts its throat. They wait a few minutes for the animal to die as the blood gushes forth and sinks into the dry ground. The higher priest then deftly slits the animal down the center on the ventral side, slits each hind leg on the inner side from the hoof to the ventral cut, and then slits the front legs in a similar manner. The priests finally wash the blood from their hands with meski, after which they drink some of the sacred beer and pour some onto the bloody ground.

Food and drink contributed by the people of the community are then placed next to the stilled sacrificial animals, and the crowd cries out a piercing "e-l-l-l-l-l-l," an age-old expression of joy in northern and central Ethiopia. Priests and elders finish butchering the animals, which are then cooked by older women past the age of menstruation. The meat is cooked in the customary chili stew and is consumed by the people with the sour, flat bread. Beer and sometimes mead (a fermented drink made with honey, water, and certain leaves used for flavoring) are dispensed from large earthenware pots holding about 25 gallons. Priests end their fast as they receive the best of the food and drink. Excess food and drink are divided among everyone to take home.

During the course of my fieldwork, in the second month of *Teqemt*, I watched daily the progress of the growing crops. At this time, Erada and his sons beam with pride at their fields and gardens, containing six-rowed barley, cabbage, lentils, peas, and shallots. The plants are ripe and ready to harvest. The skies lighten and the rains decrease to showers, as they usually do at this time of year. However, Erada and other elders of the community look apprehensively at the afternoon clouds over their fields. If heavy rains should fall, the ripening crops will be ruined. To prevent possible agricultural misfortune, the elders consult with local priests, arranging for them to hold ceremonies to regulate the rain. (In communities now lacking priests, the ceremony is often performed by Christian Qemant laymen who are knowledgeable in pagan lore.) The ceremonies in Erada's community are apparently successful, as heavy rains do not destroy the crops.

Pagan-Hebraic and Christian Qemant attend rain-regulating ceremonies in their area, each community contributing animals for the sacrifices associated with their individual ceremony. Ceremonies conducted to bring the correct amount of rain and good crops are held at various sacred sites, often at the abodes of genii loci, and may be directed to genii loci or to holy culture heroes. Ceremonies are, of course, more frequent, and attendance, especially of Christian Qemant, is larger when the rains in *Teqemt* are very heavy.

THE PERIOD OF LOCAL CEREMONIES IN THE SACRED GROVES. In the third month, *Hedar*, the hillsides of the Qemant area are, as usual, covered with an emerald mantle. The streams are high, sparkling in the golden sun, and the soil is solid and drying with the ripening crops. By this time the rains have ended. The harvest, begun in the preceding month by Erada and his sons, continues, and their labor in harvesting becomes more intensive as additional crops—broad beans, finger millet, and the oil seeds, nug, and flax—become mature. No general religious ceremony is held in *Hedar*, but some communities held ceremonies honoring their culture heroes.

The following month, *Tahsas*, has warm, dry, sunny weather and, for Erada's family and others, is a time of intensive harvesting. Crops include tef, emmer, bread-wheat, and, this year, a second crop of two-rowed barley. Erada has already harvested his first crop of two-rowed barley in the first month of *Maskaram*, and this year the soil is sufficiently moist to support a second crop. In rare years when rainfall continues into the harvest season, Erada sows a third crop of two-rowed barley after the second crop is harvested. During this month, Erada and his sons thresh and store most of the crops, and a feeling of contentment grows among them as their graneries fill. Hard work and the appropriate ritual have once again resulted in a bountiful harvest.

At this time, ceremonies are held in various communities at groves named for Keberwa, the ancestral figure of the Keber moiety. A ceremony is also held in Walaj at the grove named for Kadasti, Keberwa's brother, and in Kossoge at

A leprous minstral plays his one-stringed instrument as men harvest barley.

the grove named for Jagirho, a companion of Aydarki, who was the father of Keberwa and Kadasti.

A TIME TO ENJOY THE BOUNTY OF MEZGANA. During the fifth month, *Ter*, the expected warm and sunny weather continues; the ground is thoroughly dry and the streams become low. As the dry season progresses, the hillsides begin to yellow. Tef and chick peas are still harvested by Erada from his brown and almost barren fields, and threshing is a continued major activity. Food is plentiful, and there is leisure for rest and for visiting kith and kin who live outside the community. For Qemant, this is the time of year that makes life worth living. With a flask of beer in one hand and a large piece of bread in the other, Erada contemplates his harvested wealth and thinks of the future.

The sixth month, *Yakatit*, usually has warm, sunny weather and in some years is completely dry. There may be a few cloudy days with scattered showers and perhaps a day or two of heavy rain. These signal the beginning of the "little rains" that often extend through the next two months. The load of work during *Yakatit* is relatively light, and Erada's family now delights in consumption and gives lessening attention to production. They continue to harvest chick peas, the final crop, and begin to thresh tef. Some plowing is done for the following season; new houses are constructed and others are repaired. The leisure time and the relative prosperity after the harvest allow greater opportunities for observing rites of passage. *Tazkars* (second funerals) are common now, and all marriages take place during this season. Erada and Adonech prepare for the marriage of their youngest son, Malke. They talk of the forthcoming event constantly, and Malke begins to realize he is soon to be truly an adult and not just "little brother."

During *Yakatit*, Ethiopians who are Christians consume more meat than usual in anticipation of the fifty-five day Lenten fast. No meat or dairy products may be consumed during the fast, and no food may be taken before noon except on Saturdays and Sundays. Pagan-Hebraic Qemant do not observe the Lenten fast, and many Christian Qemant do not strictly observe it. However, the season of Christian Lent does affect, or at least coincides with, the Qemant ceremonial calendar; in the Chelga area, there are no ceremonies in sacred groves from the beginning of Lent until Passion Sunday (*Dabra Zayt*). On the day of this Christian holiday, the Qemant hold two rites of spring, or fertility ceremonies. One each is held in Karkar and in Chelga.

THE LAST JUDGMENT AND THE RITES OF SPRING. In the seventh month, *Magabit*, the mild weather continues, but the sunshine is interrupted by days with clouds and intermittent showers. Erada and his neighbors continue to construct and to repair houses and to plow their fields, but their attention is focused mainly on approaching ceremonies.

During *Magabit*, Qemant in Karkar—who are all Christian now—still celebrate an annual, but minor, fertility ceremony in the grove of Entala, the wife of Aynar, the arch-culture hero of the Qemant. Qemant say that after making a vow to Entala, "sterile women will beget children, the sick will be healed, and the poor will prosper." Entala's past position as a female spirit of fertility is indicated here. In conjunction with the ceremony of Entala, Qemant in the area

Sacrifice of a white hen during the spring fertility rite. The lower priest always holds the legs of a sacrificial animal while the higher priest slits its throat with a knife.

around Karkar prepare on the preceding Friday night for an event that is even more important than the holiday they are observing—the possible coming to earth of Mezgana for the Last Judgment (*Shamhula*). As noted in the previous discussion of *Shamhula*, it is believed this event may occur on the Sunday of Entala's ceremony (the day of *Dabra Zayt*) in any year.

In the area around Chelga, the Qemant do not knowingly observe *Shamhula*. However, on the same Friday evening before the Sunday of Entala's ceremony in Karkar, they pray and eat ceremonial bread made from chick pea flour, which for this occasion only is called *maqunen*. Although these western Qemant no longer know the reason for this ritual, it is likely that the bread was consumed as a requirement of fasting in preparation for their Last Judgment.

The ritual consumption of bread also suggests the influence of the Hebrew religion and resembles the Hebraic Passover (*Fasika*) ceremony held this time of year by the Falasha Agaw. Passover is also called *Yaqita bal* (holiday of bread) because the Falasha consume only bread (made from flour, water, and salt) and water during this holiday.

One of the most important ceremonies held among the western Qemant follows their bread ritual and falls on the same Sunday as the lesser fertility ceremony in Karkar centered upon Entala. On this day, the wambar of Chelga conducts the annual rite of spring, renewing for the coming season fertility in the fields and people. This rite appears to be ancient, existing before the Hebrew and Christian religions reached the Qemant. The original name of this ceremony or holiday has been forgotten; thus, the western Qemant call the ceremony "Dabra Zayt," the name of the Christian holiday (Passion Sunday) falling on the same day.

Although the eastern Qemant no longer hold this major fertility ceremony, they did celebrate it until a decade ago on the first day of the month of *Genbot* and called the ceremony *Fazan*. As mentioned above, they do retain remnants of a lesser fertility ceremony for Entala.

I participated in the annual fertility ceremony of the western Qemant on Sunday, March 28, 1965 (Magabit 19, 1957); the rite was held in a cluster of houses belonging to the wambar at Jalshev in Chelga. Early in the morning of this day of rest, Qemant women clean the prayer house. Food for the feast is prepared by older women who are past the age of menstruation and have undergone the rite of kasa. At about 9:00 A.M., after the preparation is finished, two priests, both standing, chant and pray for about an hour while the wambar sits silently before them. Outside, a throng of laymen gathers during the hour of audible devotions. At times during the chanting, they face the east, bow down, and rub their foreheads into and kiss the earth that is to yield their crops. At other times they hold their hands together with the palms upward, as if receiving food, while bowing down.

When the prayers are over, the priests and the wambar walk to a sacrificial area on the edge of Jalshev. The wambar's mother orders some children to bring six white chickens to the priests because the sheep they usually sacrifice are not available this year. The higher priest cuts the throats of the chickens with a knife while the lower priest holds them by the feet. Then the higher priest and the lower priest both pour some sacred beer from a large gourd onto the chicken's blood, which is soaking into the ground, and into their palms to drink. Finally, the higher priest cuts off the right leg of each chicken, and saves them for cooking in a special pot for members of the priesthood. The fast which Qemant observe on any holiday until tl e prayers and sacrifices of a ceremony are completed is then broken by the serving of a small amount of food around noon. Everyone eats a little, drinks, and talks until the ritual feast is served around 3:00 P.M. Flat bread, many varieties of chili stew, including chicken stew, and other cooked foods make up the sumptuous repast.

Following the feast, the final and most important part of the ceremony is held. Shallow baskets containing seeds of each crop are taken to a field, where prayers are said while the crowd bows to the east and kisses the ground. The priests then pray over the seeds and bless them. Next, a pair of oxen are harnessed to a plow and the wambar plows a ritual furrow in the field. He and the priests then sow some of the seeds in this furrow and pour some sacred beer over them. The Qemant assembled in the field can now eat a few of the blessed seeds remaining in the baskets. These ritual acts assure that they will be healthy and fertile. Indeed, barren women bring special offerings to the wambar at this ceremony in return for his prayers for their pregnancy and the blessed seeds which they receive.

The wambar plowing the sacred furrow in the spring fertility rite.

The following day is also a day of rest. Ritual consists of the wambar and the priests praying in a nearby grove to further insure a successful agricultural season. The fertility ceremony is now over; the annual sowing will soon begin. The prayers, the blood sacrifice, the ritual furrow with the blessed seeds, and the sacred beer have rendered the earth fertile for another season. After the ceremony is completed, Qemant say, "The yield of our crops will be certain and great."

THE TIME OF THE SOWING. During the period of my fieldwork, the eighth month, *Miyazeya*, had occasional showers (the "little rains"), and the hills in Karkar turned slightly green. Plowing and construction are continued by Erada and his neighbors in the warm and generally sunny weather. It was during this month that I tried my hand at plowing. However, when I took my position behind the plow, the two oxen threw off their yoke, looked at me, rolled their eyes, and then bolted down the hillside. The Qemant, who were too polite to tell me I smelled unnatural because of my frequent washing with soap, merely said I had frightened the animals. I then offered to help chase the beasts, but was told I had done quite enough for one day!

During *Miyazeya*, preparation is made for sowing, a time in which the men will again be working continuously from dawn to dusk. Some free time is still available, however. Sowing normally begins in this month or the next. The exact time for sowing various crops is determined by the amount of rainfall, which must be sufficient for germination. Although the fertility ceremony held the previous month insures the fruitfulness of the new crops, no Qemant in his right mind would sow before the soil is sufficiently moist.

By *Genbot*, the ninth month, the little rains are reduced to just traces of showers in the Karkar area, and the greenish hills again turn yellow as they dry. In the Chelga area, the rain has been exceptionally light for the season and none falls in *Genbot*. It is very dry and the hills are a parched brown. In both areas, the temperature ranges from very warm to hot. Construction and plowing continue, but most of the sowing, which is normally the major activity in *Genbot*, is delayed because the soil is too dry. A little sorghum, nug, and flax are sown in Chelga by the end of the month, and in Karkar, some two-rowed barley is sown.

As discussed earlier, the first day of *Genbot* marks the celebration of *Fazan*, the annual fertility ceremony in Karkar. It is now observed in only a token fashion, with some Qemant praying and serving special food in their homes. This ceremony merges with a practice of the Christian Amhara, who hold their annual commemoration of the birth of Mary on this day, and who also prepare special food and consume it with relatives and neighbors.

The lack of rain in *Genbot*, especially in Chelga, causes anxiety among both pagan-Hebraic and Christian Qemant. In the communities around Chelga, the Qemant ask their priests to hold ceremonies to regulate the rain. The wambar himself supervised two ceremonies conducted by local priests on April 27, 1965, and May 11, 1965. Sheep for the sacrifice are contributed by Qemant peasants of the area. The rites are held at a site called Adari Fardada ("The Horse of God") and consist of prayer and sacrifice conducted in a manner similar to that of the annual fertility ceremony. In this case, fewer people are present, and the sheep are consumed by the religious leaders later in the day. Other ceremonies for rain are held around this time at the abodes of genii loci in communities to the west of Chelga.

Despite the ceremonies, the dry weather continues into the middle of *Sane*, the tenth month, which is usually the first month of the big rains. By the middle of the month the rains begin, and Erada and his neighbors deem it safe to risk sowing. Plowing and house repair continue throughout this month.

During *Sane*, the wambar and priests conduct a ceremony at a holy spring (*tabal*), named Enzayimarku, in the community of Chelga. The miraculous waters of this spring are said to cure diseases and make barren women fertile. The ceremony centering on prayer and drinking of the water from the spring is on a Saturday and extends through Sunday night. Erada and other laymen who come to the spring for the ceremony pray and serve food both nights. The first of three holidays dedicated to the angel called Gargi is also held in *Sane*. These holidays are fifteen days apart.

Hamle, the eleventh month, which usually sees a daily deluge, has heavy rain approximately every other day and even less rain in the last two weeks. Erada and his three sons continue to plow and to sow daily, and the fences they had removed in the dry season are again erected to protect the sprouting crops from animals. During *Hamle*, when there is enough water to start their growth, new eucalyptus trees are usually planted. Erada already has quite a few around his house, but he plants a few more for his grandchildren. Cabbage, a home garden crop, matures and is the first food of the new season to be harvested and eaten by

Erada's family, but it is not relished by them. In fact, one time when Erada was eating with me, I served a meal of meat, potatoes, and cabbage, and he said, "Why are we eating cabbage when we have meat to eat?"

A vestigial version of the "closing ceremony" (*Balaleme*) is held on several occasions by different groups of people in Karkar. One such rudimentary observance consists of a group of ten men and women who kill a sheep and consume it with coffee made specially for the occasion. There is little praying and no chanting at this observance, which allays anxiety by having the important *Balaleme* observed in some fashion. Since there are now no priests in Karkar, the people no longer hold a large closing ceremony as they did until quite recently. The period of the "closing" of the sacred groves coincides with the wettest part of the rainy season when travel is most difficult.

The twelfth month, *Nahase*, usually has the heaviest rainfall, but it was somewhat lighter than usual during the year I spent in the field. Despite the heavy rains and leaden skies, the temperature in Karkar and Chelga rarely drops below 60°. Very wet, muddy fields are needed for the important cereal, tef, which is sown this month. Grain and oil seeds are growing and the gray-green barley, swaying in the breeze like an undulating sheet of silk, is already 2 to 3 feet high. Flax and finger millet are a few inches high, and the oil seed nug has thick, dark green shoots about 1 foot high. Potatoes are flowering, and the cabbages are thick and heavy. Qemant priests, and all other persons who have undergone the rite of kasa, fast during the entire month of *Nahase.*

Pagume is the thirteenth month and is five days long, except every fourth year, when it is six days long. During my period of fieldwork it rained only one day in *Pagume*, but the year was unusually dry. Chick peas are the only crop that has not been sown. The first crop of two-rowed barley, now turning amber, is almost ready for harvesting, but other field crops are still growing. Preharvest hunger among poorer people is lessened by potatoes, cabbages, and two-rowed barley, which can be eaten green if necessary. If the last season or two have had poor yields, a man may be forced to sell livestock in order to purchase grain to tide him over. Grain may also be borrowed from relatives and friends, if they have a surplus. Erada, however, has enough grain for consumption and enough for seed. The plowman can recall several seasons when his granaries were empty and they lived on cabbage at this time of year, but that was nothing compared to the life-taking famine in the days when his father, Aynaw, was a youth. In any event a hard life is to be preferred to no life for, as the Qemant proverb says, "A living peasant is better than a dead king."

THE NEW YEAR AND THE HARVEST. *Maskaram* is the first month of the Christian calendar and the last month of the Qemant religious cycle. The first day of this month is supposed to mark the end of the heaviest rainfall of the rainy season in northcentral Ethiopia. However, in the Qemant region, the rainy season ends in the following month, *Teqemt*; thus, the Qemant ceremonial cycle, and most likely their now-forgotten calendar, begins at this drier time. New Year's day is a time of rest for Qemant, Amhara, and Falasha, and special food is served. Erada, his family, and his neighbors eat and drink while reflecting on the past year and wondering what the future year will bring. It is also a day when zars are very active. Therefore, this is a working day for Ayo, the shaman. Among other things, he tries to learn coming events of the new year.

Squash and two-rowed barley are now being harvested, and, as enough rain is now falling, a second crop of two-rowed barley is sown by Erada and his neighbors. When it can be raised, this second crop is a boon that fills granaries and makes any preharvest hunger of the next season less severe. As the land begins to drain and dry, one is impressed by the various shades of green of the crops, the deep emerald green that has once again returned to the hills, and the wild, yellow flowers growing in profusion throughout the meadows and on the hillsides. Fields of nug are flowering in bright yellows, and the flax fields are covered with blossoms of a faded blue. In some secluded areas, thorny weeds grow with pale pink flowers. All of Qemantland looks like a picture postcard.

During this month no ceremonies are held in the sacred groves, but the wambar of Chelga observes a day of praying and feasting at his home. In the next month, *Teqemt*, the harvest is again in full swing for Erada and his neighbors, and the Qemant ceremonial cycle "opens" anew for another year. It coincides with a period of easier travel and a time of replenished food stores. Erada and his sons and grandsons look forward to another annual round of economic and ritual endeavor, just as Erada's father, Aynaw, did in his day.

9

The Life Cycle
of Mezgana's People

RITES OF PASSAGE observed by the Qemant clearly designate the various segments of their life cycle. These rites mark a transition from one period of a person's life to another and are celebrated with religious activities. Qemant rites celebrate passage into Qemant society at birth, into adulthood at marriage, into a special status as elder, and, at death, out of Qemant society and into the next world. Such rites, performed "according to Mezgana's [God's] will," bind a Qemant to his society and aid in marking the distinct social boundary between Qemant and non-Qemant. We shall now examine the way in which individual Qemant live out their lives within the structure of their society and according to the behavioral rules of their culture.

Menstruation and Childbirth Prohibitions

It is customary to begin an account of a life cycle with birth and to conclude it with death. However, the Qemant cycle of existence and related rites of passage do not end with death but instead extend beyond the grave and must be examined in that light. Similarly, to understand the beginning of the Qemant life cycle, we cannot begin with birth itself, but must first examine the Qemant view of the female as a sexually mature individual.

Qemant women are regarded as polluted and are under various taboos for one week during menstruation and after childbirth. These beliefs and customs are common to all Agaw peoples, who regard vaginal blood as being polluting and harmful. In the ritual sense, a Qemant woman is not considered absolutely clean until she has entered menopause. Once this physiological change has occurred, she may tread upon the ground of a sacred site and come in contact with ritual beverage and food.

During menstruation a Qemant woman is confined to a special menstruation hut, a permanent structure of almost every homestead. Food is brought to the woman by her family, as she may not leave the hut for any reason. On the seventh day after the onset of menses, the woman cleans the hut, washes herself and her clothing, and returns to her daily work. To me, the most striking feature of this taboo is that confinement of women during menstruation prevents their working about one-fourth of the most economically productive part of their lives. When I tried to discuss this point with male informants, they replied that women did not work very hard anyway, and when a woman is confined, her share of the work can easily be done by other women of the homestead. Apparently, Qemant men believe a woman's work is always done and she has ample time to sit down and drink beer and to gossip while spinning cotton or cooking.

Related to the menstruation taboo is a prohibition against women during childbirth. When a woman's pregnancy is well advanced, a temporary confinement hut is constructed for her in the immediate vicinity of the homestead. After the baby's birth, she retires to this hut with the new infant for seven days.

Childbirth

A woman gives birth to her first child in the house of her mother or her husband's mother, although later children may be born in her own house. To become familiar with the customary practice in childbirth among the Qemant, we shall note the procedures followed when Sahay's first child is born in the house of her husband's father and mother, Erada and Adonech:

It is a still and balmy night in the beginning of the harvest season when Sahay's labor pains begin. When the pains become acute, Adonech summons several older women from her homestead and nearby homesteads to act as midwives and to comfort Sahay during her labor. If the delivery of the child is difficult, the women may offer prayers to a culture heroine such as Entala, the wife of Aydarki. However, Sahay is a robust, sixteen-year-old girl who has no difficulty with the birth of her son. Following the delivery, Adonech cuts and ties the umbilical cord, and Erada buries the remainder of the cord and the afterbirth near the house.

The Qemant say that certain personal spirits, such as zars or personal qoles, are attracted by the cries of newborn children and hover nearby at the time of birth. Sahay is particularly worried that a potentially malevolent qole may be lingering near her new son, so Erada sacrifices a chicken to entice the spirit away from the infant. (If she so desires, the mother of the woman who has given birth may specify the color of the sacrificial chicken according to the preference of her own personal spirit.) Adonech eventually cooks the sacrificial chicken into a chili stew which is consumed with gusto by those present when the infant was born. This act has an additional benefit for those people who have assisted in the delivery. They are assured of a good meal in return for their aid and discomfort from the ritual pollution of the birth.

Following the birth of her son, Sahay goes with her infant to the confinement hut. The house where the child was delivered is then purified with a holy water (*qenona*) which has been prayed over and spat into by the wambar. The water is sprinkled around the house and on the women who took part in the birth. Before leaving the confinement hut on the seventh day, Sahay washes her body, shaves her head, and puts on clean clothing. The confinement hut is so polluted that it cannot be cleaned and reused, as can the more heavily constructed menstruation hut, and it is burned, together with Sahay's old clothing and all objects that she used while confined. Finally, Sahay is reunited with her husband, Bitaw.

After leaving the confinement hut, the infant is circumcised, and Erada, the proud grandfather, sacrifices another chicken. Circumcision is a custom followed by most Cushitic-speaking peoples. Among the Qemant this custom is observed on the eighth day after birth, in accordance with ancient Hebraic practice. An iron knife or razor is used to circumcise both males and females, although the operation on females might be better termed excision of the clitoris.

Qenona, the Rite of Passage into Qemant Society

Qemant infants are initiated into society twenty to thirty days after birth by a rite called *qenona*. The wambar usually gives permission for the ceremony, although he need not be present. The new son of Sahay and Bitaw is no exception to the rule, and is therefore bathed in a large wooden bowl of holy *qenona* water while a priest offers prayers. When the infant is lifted from the bowl and given new clothing, he is considered a member of Qemant society. The child is then given several names. One of these is his "religious name," which is used in ceremonies and symbolizes his new status as a person. Sahay and Bitaw decide that the infant's common name should be Waldu.

Qenona is basically a rite of purification, accomplished by use of holy water. It is not an imitation of baptism, although some Christian Amhara regard it as such. The holy water ritually cleanses an infant for admittance to Qemant society. Adults may also be cleansed by the same rite when they become polluted. Such cases include men who slaughter animals on days when it is forbidden (Wednesdays, Fridays, and Saturdays), women who leave the menstruation hut before seven days have passed, women who are not confined for seven days after giving birth, and anyone who has been bitten by a hyena. Muslims or Christians may become Qemant by undergoing this rite of passage into Qemant society, but none have been known to do so.

Until a few decades ago, the visit of a non-Qemant to a Qemant household required a *qenona* rite to purify the area and all utensils touched by the "unclean one." Before the rite was performed, the women of the family swept the house and washed everything the alien had touched. These beliefs and practices isolated the Qemant, preventing completely the formation of bonds of friendship with non-Qemant or any close social contact with outsiders. The social boundary erected by these ideas of ritual pollution began to break down after the conversion of some Qemant to Christianity in the 1880s. Bonds of kinship played a role in weakening the old ideas of exclusiveness; aversion to ritual pollution through contact with people of other religions was less when these people were kinsmen and old friends who had become Christians.

Contact with the Mother and Body Covering

Qemant children are nursed until approximately two years of age, by which time they are usually walking and talking. During the period of nursing, a child derives a sense of security and well-being from much close contact with the mother's body. Some Qemant mothers let their children whimper and scream for a time before nursing them, but most infants are allowed to crawl around inside their mother's clothing and can therefore nurse at will. This is the case with Waldu, the pampered one. He is also carried on the back of Sahay, his mother, or that of another female relative, in a leather carrier until he is approximately two years of age. The carrier is used while the women travel, work about the house, and labor in the fields.

The Qemant have a saying that "love goes downward," meaning that when a new child is born, parents and kin decrease displays of affection for older children in order to accommodate the infant's need for love. After a sibling is born, or a child reaches three years of age, bodily contact with the mother and nursing are ended. Weaning may be gradual or abrupt. Bitter herbs or manure may be rubbed on the nipples to discourage a child from nursing and forced abstinence may be employed. A child receives solid foods toward the end of the period of breast feeding, but is not given spicy or peppery food.

Weaning is a traumatic experience for the child, especially if a younger rival is present. The child feels banished from its mother's warmth and love. Now put to bed with older siblings, the child often tries to climb back into the mother's garments or into the carrier on her back, even when an infant sibling is there. An infant is completely covered by its mother's clothing while sleeping. When the child has begun to sleep alone, the mother sees that it is wrapped from head to foot in a toga or other adult garment. Older children and adults wrap themselves completely from head to foot in bedclothes of woven cotton when they retire, a habit that is a continuation of this practice of the first few years whereby one is completely covered while sleeping.

Early Training

The early training of a Qemant child is exemplified by the "torments" experienced by four-year-old Tadasa, the third son of Nagash, Bitaw's older brother. While Tadasa is being weaned, a small basket of food is placed before him, and older siblings and his doting grandmother, Adonech, teach him the motor habits of eating. Like other very young children, Tadasa is given much cow's milk and other dairy products. In addition to regular meals, he is fed at various other times during the day, especially if he asks or cries for food.

During the period of weaning, Tadasa receives intensive training in etiquette, learning actions of respect, such as kissing the knee of an elder, and verbal formulas such as "good day" (*tenalayen*) and "thank you" (*Adaralayen*). Young children like Tadasa and Waldu are allowed to walk and to crawl about the house, but may not destroy things. Punishment for misbehavior is sometimes verbal; Tadasa and his older brothers, Guwalu and Warqe, are scolded or threatened. Common threats for Tadasa include: "A hyena will get you," or "A stranger will harm you." At other times, his parents may pinch him, slap him, or withhold his food. Food and drink are sometimes used as bribes to make the three brothers behave.

Young boys and girls are not segregated. Tadasa plays and fights with girls as well as boys, but sexual play between them is not permitted; in older children it is punished. After puberty, boys and girls no longer sleep together. Boys usually gain sexual knowledge gradually from listening to conversations of young men. Talking about sex in the house or at mixed gatherings is considered improper.

Training in cleanliness is an important part of the education of Qemant children. Tadasa is taught to wash his hands before eating or helping to prepare food. By slapping Tadasa's left hand, Warqe reminds him that only the right hand may be used for removing food from the basket used as a table at mealtime. The left hand, which is often used in the discharge of body wastes, may be used when necessary to hold food after it is removed from the basket. Children are also taught to wash their clothing once or twice a month.

Tadasa and Waldu are not trained strictly about when and where they may defecate and urinate. Because he is under two years of age, Waldu is not scolded for doing either in the house. Later, he must go outside, as Tadasa does, increasing the distance from the house as he gets older. Adolescents and adults may urinate in the area around a house, although they may not defecate there and must use the fields instead.

Occupational Role Training

Preparation for occupational roles is an important part of the child's training. In childhood, much of this preparation is in the form of play. Tadasa and Guwalu construct small houses of sticks and mud, play horsemen while astride a stick, and practice plowing. Guwalu uses a stick for the plowshaft and Tadasa as the ox. Tadasa tells Waldu he will someday hitch him to the plow. "Do so and I shall pinch your cheek," warns grandmother Adonech. Miniature oxen whips made of wood and bark are also playthings for the boys. Some boys such as Warqe become shepherds at five years of age and receive "on-the-job training" from older boys. It is not unusual to see a little shepherd weighing only about 40 pounds beating an ox of almost 1 ton across the shin with a very thin stick, usually to no avail. Such training usually begins during the harvest, when the neighbor's fields are full of potential food in the form of growing crops. The young shepherds help themselves to any of the edible plants when

Herding of livestock is work for boys. Cattle are mixed breeds of zebu and other types.

the owner of the crops is not around. This is an attraction of the job, which serves to break the young boy away from his mother and the hearth. Although, Warqe, whose name means gold, is now twelve years of age, he still helps himself to his neighbors' crops. One irate tiller of the soil mutters, "I put up fences to keep the livestock from eating my crops, but Warqe climbs over them like a monkey. He will need more than a golden name to compensate me."

Young girls "grind" dirt between two stones and prepare "meals" of mud. Beginning around three years of age, they chase chickens away from food and fetch implements and firewood. A year or two later, they run errands to neighboring homesteads.

When children are about eight years of age, they begin to assist their parents in all tasks. Girls grind grain, wash clothing, clean the house, and prepare food, though they are not entrusted to cook meals with costly foods, such as meat stew. Boys assist their fathers at the market, in constructing houses, and in the fields. Occasionally, as a father will, Nagash allows Warqe to take out the oxen and plow for a "spin" around a nearby field. By middle and late adolescence, boys and girls know how to perform with skill all life's tasks. For the welfare of the parents as well as of the children, parents should train children thoroughly in the roles of adult life, for security in old age is provided by strong, capable sons and married daughters. Nagash, Bitaw, and Malke, their youngest son, have begun to provide such security for Erada and his wife. Aided by his three strapping sons, Erada can effectively cultivate more of the land that he claims through ambilineal descent links. The increased agricultural yield results in greater wealth and power for Erada than he would have with only one son to help him, or, perish the thought, none at all.

Clothing and Adornment

Until they reach five or six years of age, Qemant children like Tadasa and Waldu are permitted to be nude part of the time, but after this age they must always wear clothing. Young children often wear one-piece garments that are open on the bottom, simple dresses for girls and long shirts for boys. Warqe and his older male relatives wear a long shirt with shorts or riding breeches or long trousers held up with a belt or cord. Headgear is not common. A long white toga is wrapped over the clothing and may be used in place of or in addition to a shirt by adult males. Cloaks of animal skins and blankets may also be wrapped around the body. Adonech and her daughters-in-law wear a long, one-piece dress with a sash tied around the center, and they may wear a toga over the dress. The dress and the toga sometimes have colored, hand-embroidered designs on the border. Sandals of leather, or, in recent years, sandals made in Gondar from old truck tires, are used by some people.

Personal ornaments for young children consist of necklaces of beads of blue glass and of seashells. Girls and women also wear bands of copper or silver and small strands of blue glass beads as both bracelets and anklets. Either sex may wear rings of copper or silver. Pendants of Ethiopian, and sometimes British or Italian, coins may be worn on a chain or cord around the neck; small leather cases in which amulets are carried may also be worn on this cord.

Women's ears are pierced for small, circular earrings of silver. Fifty years ago some men also wore earrings. Tattooing is a common form of adornment and is done on the upper gums, neck, chest, forehead, hand, lower forearm, and ankles. Nug oil and soot are heated together to make a dark blue dye for the tattoos, which are done by puncturing the skin repeatedly with the thorns of a variety of acacia tree dipped into the pigment. In addition to being decorative, tattoos serve therapeutic and protective functions. When on the neck, they are said to cure goiter, and when on the gums, to stop toothaches. Tattooing on girls such as Sahay and her sister-in-law Almaz wards off the evil eye that is said to afflict attractive females.

There are no special hair styles for very young children like Waldu. As is customary for boys four or five years of age, Tadasa's head is shaved except for a long central scalp lock. When he is about ten years of age, his head will be completely shaved like Warqe's is now. Nagash and his brothers keep their hair short, as is common for men eighteen years of age and over. Some older men like Erada have long, bushy hair in a style formerly used by warriors during times of war such as the period from 1935 to 1941.

When a girl is about four years of age, her hair is allowed to grow long and is made up into numerous small braids, except for a circular, shaven spot over the upper part of the back of the head. When she is approximately eight years of age, a girl's hair is cut short, but the shaved area is retained. After several years of marriage, a girl's hair is allowed to grow long again, covering the shaved area, and is worn in many small braids. An old woman wears her hair very short, in a style similar to that of a man. This style is also worn by women in mourning.

Styles of clothing, hair, and ornaments are the same for the Qemant, Amhara, and Falasha of Bagemder and Semen.

Marriage and Adulthood

In order to understand Qemant marriage in particular, we shall later attend the marriage ceremony uniting pretty Kababush and Malke, Erada's youngest son and the "little brother" of Nagash and Bitaw. Let us first examine Qemant marriage in general. Girls marry when they are very young, sometimes at seven years of age, but usually between eight and fifteen. Premarital sexual relations are rare for a girl, and virginity is the ideal for unmarried girls. Unless she is marrying for the second time, a girl cannot easily get a husband if she is not a virgin. Among women, such forbidden sexual relations as occur are usually extramarital and provide grounds for divorce. Pregnancy before marriage is highly improper and rarely occurs. Because the age of marriage is early, women seldom, in any case, bear children until some years after marriage.

Concubinage is permitted, but is uncommon; it usually occurs when a man has a wife who has not yet reached puberty. Since a very poor girl has little opportunity to marry because she lacks sufficient wealth to make a contribution to the marriage and a family of sufficient prestige, she may become a servant in a wealthy household. It is permissible for her to have a child by one of the married or unmarried sons of the household employing her. Should she eventually leave the household, the child usually remains with the father. Formerly, when slavery existed, a man was permitted to have sexual relations with a slave. Prostitution is unknown among the Qemant.

Men usually marry when eighteen to twenty years of age, but their age at marriage extends up to thirty. Opportunities for men to have premarital sexual relations are limited, but occur occasionally with older married and divorced women and widows. Rape is rare among the Qemant. Homosexual relationships sometimes exist among boys while they are shepherds.

Qemant marriages are customarily arranged by an oral contract between the parents of the prospective bride and groom. Use rights to land and other wealth of the families of the bride and the groom are taken into consideration in the marriage contract and are usually the measure of wealth used in arranging marriages. Marriage (*fahu yewinat*), and the marriage ceremony (*senaw*), constitute a rite of passage from adolescence to young adulthood for Qemant males. This is not always the case for females because of their youth. There is no other coming-of-age ceremony for males or females.

Transfers of Wealth in Marriage

The families of the bride and groom each make a contribution (*macha*) in money and livestock, which the couple uses jointly in its married life. Amounts are specified in the oral marriage contract. If one spouse brings a larger amount than the other, the difference usually remains his, or her, property and is retained if divorce ensues.

Vestiges remain of a custom of paying a bride price (*mataya*), which ranges from seven and one-half Ethiopian paper dollars to twenty Maria Theresa silver dollars. If the bride comes from a wealthy family, the amount is usually above the minimum. The prospective groom and his father give the money to the bride's parents, but the bride's parents then give it to the newlyweds in one of two ways. After the wedding feast, the groom may sing songs of war in front of the house of the bride's parents, after which they give him the money as a reward for his "excellent and warriorlike singing." Sometimes the bride's parents add extra money or goods. In the other instance, the bride's father buys a new mat of cowhide, which is used to sit on, and various other articles for the young couple's household or for the bride's personal use. The articles are presented in a basket with a leather covering. If the money is not adequate to cover the cost, the bride's father may add some of his own money. It may be assumed that the bride price was greater at one time and that the Qemant formerly used it to transfer wealth and to insure that the bonds of marriage would be strong. The bride price now consists principally of a mutual exchange of good will that solidifies ties between the two families.

Very rarely, a man and his friends abduct a girl and force a marriage. This may occur when a father does not want his daughter to marry a certain man, sometimes because the man is poor. Qemant priests and elders prevent abductions from leading to strife by levying upon the abductor a fine in cattle or money, which gives redress and prestige to the father in the eyes of the community. The fine is seldom actually a transfer of wealth or a form of punishment since the father usually returns the fine to the couple. It is instead a means of keeping peace by ritually compensating the father for his loss.

Civil and Religious Marriage

The Qemant are united in marriage by civil or religious ceremonies. A third kind of union also exists in which a couple may simply live together. This arrangement is often of short duration and may be dissolved at any time by either party.

The civil marriage is for laymen and is marked with a marriage feast, but there is no religious observance. A couple may be divorced at any time by mutual agreement; their common property is then divided equally. However, if such a couple reaches old age and both undergo the rite of passage (*kasa*) marking the status of elder, they may not be divorced. If a couple undergoes this ritual and one spouse subsequently dies, the other spouse must gain permission from the wambar to remarry. The new spouse must then undergo the same ritual, if he, or she, has not already done so.

Religious marriage among the Qemant is for members of the priesthood only and is thus rare. A priest first receives permission to marry from the wambar.

He then goes with other priests to the house of his prospective bride. There, in a ceremony conducted by other priests, he swears to respect his new wife and not to divorce her. The girl then undergoes the rite of *kasa*. Although a priest has already undergone this rite at his ordination, he does so again at his marriage ceremony. A marriage feast follows. Upon the death of his wife, a priest may marry a second time, but only with the wambar's permission.

The ceremony of a civil marriage is described below. Rites of a religious marriage are very similar and differ only in the addition of the religious observances described previously.

The Marriage of Malke and Kababush

Today Malke, a handsome young man twenty years of age, marries Kababush, a charming and shy girl ten years of age. Soon after dawn, we find Malke and his party, resplendent in new white clothing, winding along the trails to the homestead of the parents of Kababush. Accompanying Malke are his kin and his mizes, eight fictive siblings he selected sometime before his marriage (see Chapter 6).

Arriving at the homestead, Malke and his party find a beehive of activity. Hay and leaves are being strewn upon the ground beneath a large canopy made of boughs placed on poles which was erected three days before to shelter the wedding guests. The rich aroma of baking bread mingles in the air with the spicy bouquet of bubbling chili stews being prepared by the women of Kababush's family. Dogs are gathered in the far corner of the homestead to scavenge the remnants of a cow being slaughtered by the men. Part of the beef is cut up and added to the stews, part is saved to be consumed raw, and the undesirable portions are left for the drooling dogs, whose eyes are riveted to the animal's carcass. The beating wings of descending vultures add the final touch to this grisly scene of carnage so markedly in contrast to the rest of the wedding activities.

High-pitched, wailing notes from a one-stringed, violinlike instrument belonging to a wandering minstrel provide a musical background for Malke and two of his mizes as they wait in front of the house of the bride's parents. The two companions are called "father" (*aba*) mize and "servant" (*ashkar*) mize. The father mize, who is the oldest member of the mize group, serves as an advisor to the groom. The servant mize, who is the youngest member of the group, serves food and drink to the bride at the wedding. The two men are presented to the father of Kababush, who ritually asks: "Tell me who the mizes are; who will be responsible for Kababush; who will advise her; who will encourage her; who will hear her secrets?" Malke then introduces the men to the father of the bride. The two mizes step behind a curtain with Kababush and the three drink beer from the same cup, vowing meanwhile to treat each other like brother and sister.

The ceremony of civil marriage then continues inside the house of the bride's parents. The rite of marriage itself is very brief. The oral marriage contract, previously completed by the two families, is recited. Kababush, who is completely covered by a finely woven white toga, and Malke swear that each is the spouse of the other.

The secular observance is followed by the wedding feast, held under the great canopy. Fragrant eucalyptus leaves covering the ground scent the air. The festivities will continue into the next day, when Kababush will make her first appearance in public. Today, however, she is guarded inside her father's house by the mizes, who feed her, talk and joke with her, and are the only persons allowed to see her. Malke and his family remain with the guests throughout the night, while eating and drinking continue. Music and songs are performed by the minstrel, whose unsteady locomotion reflects the state of many of the merrymakers.

In the middle of the second day, one of the mizes collects money from the guests for the bride and groom. A little later, another mize wraps Kababush in a toga and carries her outside her father's house. She is placed next to Malke on a new mat of cowhide under the canopy of boughs, and the mizes enertain the couple. Two mizes begin to dance, facing one another and moving only their shoulders to the sonorous beat of a drum. After this they sing songs of valor in war. Malke then stands and sings songs of warfare and receives from the bride's father his "reward" of the bride price for his proficient singing and arrogant, warriorlike demeanor. This custom is a survival from the past, when a young man had to demonstrate his prowess as a warrior before he was accepted as an adult and allowed to take a wife. The Qemant today face no threats of war and no longer test their young men in their ability as warriors, but this vestige of the test is repeated at every wedding.

Late in the afternoon Malke and the mizes transport Kababush over hill and dale to the homestead of Malke's parents. Kababush is carried on the back of a mize, although a mule could be used instead. Kababush is at this time still wrapped in her white toga so that no one can see her, especially people with the evil eye. Upon their arrival, all the mizes and Malke drink beer from the same cup and swear friendship. All of the mizes vow to treat the couple like brother and sister and to address them as such when speaking. The mizes are subsequently to be the fictive brothers of the bride and groom and may be asked to settle quarrels between them.

Adulthood and Married Life

If a girl is past puberty at the time of her marriage, she usually resides with the groom at his father's house. In this case the marriage would have been consummated on the night following the end of the marriage feast. In such instances one of the older mizes sometimes helps the groom by deflowering his bride, or at least by offering this service and any advice needed on sexual matters. The bride may, however, follow the custom of residence observed by most younger girls. If a girl marries before reaching puberty, the marriage is not consummated until she matures. This is the case with Malke and his new bride. Kabakush continues to live with her parents, while Malke lives with his parents. Kababush comes to live with the groom's parents for periods of a week or a month at a time, prolonging the visits as she matures. During this time Malke continues to sleep alone.

The child bride works alongside Adonech, her mother-in-law, and the wives of Malke's brothers. From these women, Kababush learns culinary arts and other duties of the household as these are customarily performed in her husband's family, the social unit in which she will spend the rest of her life. As time passes, a bond is gradually formed between the young bride and her husband's family. The pain of leaving her natal family is lessened, and her residence with them eventually ends. Kababush thus faces no sudden plunge into new and unfamiliar surroundings and procedures. Her gradual introduction to marriage is also helpful to the groom and other members of his family, easing anxiety and tensions between the bride and groom and between the bride and her affinal kin.

The marriage of a child bride is consummated after puberty, generally when a girl is about thirteen years old. For consummation of the marriage, the young couple usually retires to a hut or to a secluded area. If the girl marries before reaching puberty, an oral contract may be made between her parents and the parents of the groom stipulating the length of time that must expire before the marriage is consummated. Such contracts usually designate a time shortly after the beginning of menses, and may provide that if the couple has sexual relations before the stipulated time resulting in physical injury to the girl, a sum of money must be paid to the girl's parents. If physical injury is not severe, the provisions of the contract are generally not enforced. When injury is severe, the girl's parents hold the money in trust for her in case she is ever divorced by her husband.

A woman's first pregnancy may come at about fifteen years of age. The expectant mother works as usual until pregnancy is well advanced, when she performs only light tasks. Male children are usually preferred for economic reasons. Infanticide is not practiced, even when children are deformed. Abortion is known but not condoned. Contraception is also disapproved, but some women make brews of certain herbs that they drink in unsuccessful attempts to prevent conception.

After several years of marriage, a couple builds its own house and sets up a household next to that of the groom's parents. The couple gives notice of its new status by following Qemant rules of hospitality. According to Qemant belief, every house belongs to Mezgana, and hospitality should ideally be extended to all Qemant, even those who are strangers. The visitor should be invited in, and given food and drink after the host washes his feet. In practice, few people get their feet wet in this manner, and beggars who approach a house are usually given a handful of food and sent on their way. The realities of the peasant economy usually discourage any greater charity. Invited guests, however, are fed special pieces of food by the host's hand and are urged to eat and drink to the bursting point.

The Status of Venerated Elder and *Kasa*

During most of the years of their adult life, Qemant men and women devote their time and efforts principally to wresting a livelihood from the environment and to rearing children. When they are about fifty years of age, however, they take on new statuses and roles as elders. Qemant value the opinions of elders in judicial matters, and younger adults seek their advice in matters concerning family and agriculture. Qemant believe that they will be rewarded in the next life if they respect and heed their elders.

As noted earlier in discussing judicial procedures, attainment of the status of venerated elder may be marked with a rite of passage (*kasa*). Most but not all elders undergo this ceremony, which is regarded as being equally as important as the rites at childbirth and marriage. To qualify, a man must be old enough to have gray hair and a woman must be beyond menstruation. It is assumed that such an elder is "too old to sin any longer." Any elder of either sex who has undergone this ritual may not enter a place where women are menstruating, may not obtain a divorce, and may partake only of food and beverage prepared by a pagan-Hebraic Qemant. In this manner, a person retains a nearer-to-Mezgana purity.

To become a venerable elder, Erada had to undergo a rite called *yaqum tazkar* before the rite of *kasa*; the two ceremonies were held on the same day. The *yaqum tazkar* is a rite which everyone eventually undergoes before death; it prepares the way to heaven for a respected and honored elder and emphasizes his or her close proximity to the Qemant pantheon. The ceremony for Erada consisted of prayers by local priests and blessings by relatives and neighbors, followed by a feast Erada provided for the participants. If poor, an elder may give a small feast for the priests only. (Priests undergo a *yaqum tazkar* at their ordination to demonstrate that they maintain this closeness to Mezgana even in their youth.)

The subsequent ceremony of *kasa* for Erada was comprised of prayers and chanting on his behalf by priests and ended after Erada drank, for the first time in his life, sacred beer served in a special gourd cup. When Erada and other venerated elders who have undergone *kasa* participate in the various rites, they customarily drink sacred beer.

The Lamentation, the Rite of Passage from Qemant Society

Among the Qemant, death requires two observances, a rite of "lamentation" (*laqso*) to usher the deceased out of human society, and a rite in "commemoration of the deceased" (a *tazkar*) to send his soul to the other world. The lamentation, held on the day of burial, may be considered the funeral, and the commemoration of the deceased, held a few months later, may be considered the second funeral. Qemant attribute death to injury or disease, and do not believe that it results from old age. Disease is usually said to be caused by supernatural beings such as zars, Saytan, or people with the evil eye. Sometimes the death of the rare person who knows how to read is said to have come from the supernatural power of the written words. Such a death is considered to be self-inflicted but not intentional or suicidal.

A person who commits suicide is not given rites of lamentation or commemoration and is not interred in sacred ground because it is felt that he brought about death before its proper time. Qemant also believe that suicide is the most antisocial of all acts because it disavows the sacredness of life and frees a person from his societal restraints and obligations. The two rites are also not held for a woman who dies during menstruation. Her body is interred near but outside the boundaries of a sacred burial grove so that she will not pollute the grove.

On a clear, cool morning during the sowing season, the rite of lamentation is nearing for Aynaw, the elderly father of Erada the plowman and Ayo the shaman. The patriarch lies near death, and Kababush is sent to summon a priest who comes to pray for him. The priest is among those who hear Aynaw recite his last will and testament. Aynaw dies in the afternoon amidst his grief-stricken family. That evening, in preparation for burial his corpse is washed, and his eyes and the mouth are closed so that his face will have a "natural" appearance. Aynaw's corpse is then placed in a supine position. Its hands are tied to the front of the thighs, and the thumbs are tied together. The big toes are also tied together. The body is finally wrapped completely in a piece of white cloth and then in a mat of woven grass. Wambars receive the same preparation, but are then placed into a box made from the wood of trees from a sacred grove. When a person dies in the morning, burial usually follows on the same day. However, because Aynaw's death occurs in the afternoon, interment is on the following morning.

Aynaw's relatives and friends, who live some distance from his homestead, are notified of the funeral, or rite of lamentation, throughout the night by long, drawn out, falsetto shouting from hilltops. The morning after the message is delivered, long lines of wailing mourners, dressed in special white clothing used for holidays, are seen winding over the hills and through the shadowy valleys. The mourners gather in the area of Erada's homestead, and the air is filled with their wails and laments. Consanguineal and affinal relatives (by blood and by marriage) of the deceased appear extremely grief stricken. In their bereavement many relatives shave their heads and slash the skin on their cheeks with fingernails.

Aynaw's remains are placed on a litter and carried to a sacred burial grove with the procession of mourners following. When the procession reaches the burial grove, the people form a circle around the immediate relatives of Aynaw and his closest friends. The relatives and friends then hold up implements and clothing which belonged to the patriach, lamenting, "Aynaw has left his home, his family, his property, and all his worldly pleasures and will never again use these articles." The throng continues to weep and wail.

Aynaw is then buried in a shallow grave within the sacred burial grove.

The body is placed on its right side with the soles of the feet toward the east. Qemant maintain that the corpse is now "facing east," the direction faced when praying. The shallow grave is filled with earth and then topped with stones. Since Aynaw has undergone the rite of *kasa*, priests deliver prayers at the interment, and, after the burial, they bless the grave and pour sacred beer over it. People who have not undergone the rite of *kasa* do not receive a religious observance at their funerals.

After the burial, the mourners return to the houses of Erada and Ayo to share a final bit of sorrow with the family and perhaps to allay further their own anxieties about death. Relatives from outlying areas may stay as long as three days. Food supplied by neighbors, relatives who live nearby, and fellow members of associations is served to all mourners.

The *Tazkar*, the Second Funeral

A person's final rite of passage, the second funeral (*tazkar*), is held for him by his or her spouse, if living, and children anytime within a few months after the funeral. Qemant say this rite is for commemoration of the deceased and allows a person to enter heaven and be content beyond the grave. The rite appears to be very ancient among the Agaw and can be regarded as pre-Christian in origin. Among the ancestral Agaw, the *tazkar* may formerly have been a second funeral held to assure that the potentially dangerous soul of the decreased had actually left the natural world and entered the supernatural world. An archaic survival of the rite is found among the Qemant, but it also survives as part of the Hebraic (Falasha) and Christian (Amhara) religious rituals found in Ethiopia.

Almost everyone in a Qemant community attends a second funeral. In the ceremony, priests pray to gods of the Qemant pantheon, asking that the soul be allowed to reach heaven. Everyone then takes part in a large feast provided by the family of the deceased. The guests say, "Let Mezgana have mercy upon his soul," which signifies that the members of the community agree that the soul should enter the next world. The priests and guests then bless the family and, after further feasting, the ceremony ends.

One of the largest and most important second funerals in several decades was held in February 1965, for Marsha Zawdu, the father of the present wambar, Mulunah Marsha. Marsha Zawdu, who died in November of 1964, was a de facto wambar after the death of the wambar of Chelga in 1941. The ceremony was celebrated in two parts, the first for Christian Qemant and the second for pagan-Hebraic Qemant. Let us now observe both parts of the greatest *tazkar* Qemantland had seen in many years:

The first part of the ceremony begins on a Sunday and will continue into the next day. Many hundreds of Christian Qemant attend this event, celebrated at the homestead of the present wambar at Jalshev. The people assembled on this day are noted to resemble "a throng gathered on a great market day."

Feasting at the tazkar of the father of the wambar of Chelga.

Six oxen are slaughtered for the feast, during which the assembled Christian Qemant ritually say, "Let Mezgana have mercy upon Marsha."

Wednesday evening marks the beginning of the second part of the ceremony in which only pagan-Hebraic Qemant can participate. About eighty laymen and eight priests are there, some from communities more distant than a day's walk. The wambar, the priests, and persons who have undergone the rite of *kasa* enter a large circular hut made of boughs and specially constructed for the event. Others wait outside. The priests pray and chant, and then food is served to everyone. Food for those inside the hut is prepared separately, cooked in the doorway of the hut. In the center of the hut there are gourds containing sacred beer behind a small screen of cloth, which shields the sacred beverage from people who have not undergone *kasa*. The sacred beer is served to those inside the hut by a guardian of the sacred beverage.

A second ceremony is held in the hut on the following morning around 8:00 A.M. Praying and chanting by eight priests from four communities in the western Qemant area is conducted by the wambar. Mezgana, Keberwa, and the ark of the covenant of Moses are mentioned in the prayers, which concern the welfare of the living Qemant as well as the soul of the deceased father of the wambar. The priests and the people face the east with their palms upward in supplication and bow deeply so that their foreheads are pressed to the ground as the praying ends with a chant by the priests. Finally, in a sacrificial area nearby, a higher priest slaughters a bellowing ox and three bleating sheep while a lower priest holds the legs of the animals. The ensuing feast lasts the rest of the day and into the following afternoon. Approximately 200 gallons of beer, 20 gallons of mead, and hundreds of flat breads are consumed with the beef and mutton.

This evening a special subceremony called *warabe* is performed. The event includes unique chanting in which the priests sing a refrain with one priest leading the singing. Ceremonial dancing follows in which two priests chant and dance in small steps in a circle three meters in diameter. Now and then the dancing priests call out the name of a female venerable elder who has undergone *kasa* and she then steps forward and joins in the dance. As each woman finishes dancing, she bows very low to the gourds of sacred beer behind the screen. Mead which has been specially blessed is served after the ceremony. The priests and laymen drink and talk for the rest of the night. There is no further ceremony, but feasting continues on into the next day. The signal for us to disband is the pouring onto the ground of the thick cereal residue in the great empty beer pots. This act is equivalent to our emptying the ashtrays to give the hint that the party is over. People begin to leave Jalshev around noon and by dusk, everyone has departed.

Priests hold a prayer ceremony (*amatat*) on the annual anniversary of each person's second funeral. This ceremony, which is held in the grove where the person is buried, is ideally continued for several decades after a person's death. It preserves in memory former Qemant who have lived their lives as Mezgana's people in accord with his commandments, the basic behavioral rules of Qemant society.

10

Cultural Change and the Qemant

THE ROLE OF THE QEMANT RELIGION, with its associated boundary-maintaining mechanisms, in the process of acculturation called Amharization is examined in this concluding chapter. The societal boundary-maintaining mechanisms of the Qemant may be considered a form of cultural adaptation to the sociocultural environment. In the same manner in which technology and supernaturalism enable the Qemant to survive privation and apprehension stemming from the vicissitudes of their geographical environment, this adaptation allowed them to survive acculturation for centuries while encircled by the dominant Amhara. Nevertheless, the process of Amharization is finally bringing to an end the Qemant society and culture. Reasons for the current demise of the Qemant and their way of life, despite the existence of cultural boundaries preventing change, will be examined. Cultural change among the Qemant, it may be added, is here considered as a process of acculturation that is not Westernization. Finally, Amharization is viewed in the light of its effect on Ethiopian peoples other than the Qemant.

Amharization of the Qemant may be divided into three phases, which I shall call initial, maximal, and terminal. Before elaborating on each stage of Amharization, a brief outline of the entire process is presented here. The initial phase of Amharization was of moderate intensity and began around A.D. 1270, when the Amhara became the rulers of Abyssinia. After this time, the Qemant and the Amhara had considerable first-hand contact with one another, but the Qemant long maintained their social identity, and the rate of Amharization was minimal.

Initial Amharization of the Qemant ended late in the nineteenth century when Emperor Johannes IV of Abyssinia carried out a program of forced Amharization in order to unify his culturally diverse nation and thereby to withstand outside military pressures on Abyssinia. The maximal phase of Amharization of the Qemant had begun. The changes in culture engendered by the emperor had greater effect on the Qemant than on other peoples in Abyssinia, irreparably rupturing their societal boundaries, which had been preserved in large part by beliefs and practices of their pagan-Hebraic religion.

Forced Amharization was re-emphasized after World War II. This program gave the coup de grace to the Qemant sociocultural system, which then entered the terminal, or final, phase of Amharization.

Initial Amharization and Stabilized Pluralism

Amharization of the Qemant, and other enclaves of the Agaw, is a continuation of acculturation that began when the proto-Amhara came into contact with the Agaw south of the Takaze River around A.D. 1000. As already noted in Chapter 2, the resulting process of acculturative fusion gradually changed to acculturative assimilation by the Amhara as the influence of the Agaw declined and their population decreased. This assimilation, which I call Amharization, was to become complete for many groups of Agaw by the end of the fifteenth century.

In a few areas, Amharization was very slow, and some Agaw groups became culturally distinct enclaves within the expanding Amhara population. In such cases, the Agaw and the neighboring Amhara formed what may be described as regional areas of stabilized plural societies. Factors responsible for the slow rate of acculturation differed from one area to another. Terrain was a barrier against Amharization of Agaw groups in mountainous areas such as Semen and Lasta. Agaw in Qwara were able to preserve their culture because they were remote from centers of Amhara power. In areas such as Semen, Lasta, and Agawmeder, the Agaw were able to resist Amharization for centuries, often by use of armed force.

Long before widespread Amharization of the Agaw came about, the pagan-Hebraic religion of the Qemant had differentiated them from their adversaries, Agaw groups with religions that were markedly Hebraic and included relatively few pagan elements. The Qemant developed nascent mechanisms that opposed acculturation by the Hebraic Agaw. Without these, the Qemant might easily have been assimilated by these Agaw, who were otherwise closely similar, inhabited contiguous areas, and were far more numerous. Qemant defense mechanisms were further developed as the dominance of the encircling Amhara waxed, and these defenses arrested the rate of progressive adjustment leading to Amharization. This allowed the Qemant and Amhara cultures to exist in a relationship of stabilized societal pluralism. Thus, the Qemant did not lose their cultural identity as did many other Agaw peoples in contact with the Amhara.

In the centuries before the beginning of European contact with Abyssinia (around 1500), Amharization of most of the Agaw groups proceeded at an ever-increasing rate, in spite of opposition from the Agaw and other inhibiting factors. We do not know exactly when the Qemant became politically subordinate to the Amhara, but it must have been well before the early seventeenth century, when the Amhara built their first permanent capital, Gondar, in the midst of their Qemant vassals, who supported the town. The Qemant provided a reservoir of labor, and provided agricultural products and fuel for Gondar. Most early European accounts state that little could be learned about the

Qemant save that they then performed the important but degrading tasks of providing firewood, water, and animal fodder for Gondar. Without this fuel, the capital would probably not have been permanent, for it is known that Ethiopian towns could not long endure without a supply of fuel from the hinterland.

In contrast with most other Agaw groups, the Qemant offered no resistance to the Amhara. This fact is evident from information contained in Qemant oral traditions and in Amhara chronicles, which do not mention strife between the two peoples, but do note warfare between the Amhara and other Agaw. The Qemant simply submitted and paid their taxes. Thus, it was not necessary for the Amhara to destroy the politicoreligious system of the Qemant in order to subjugate them. Perhaps the Qemant felt that Amhara control would give them some protection from the other, more Hebraized groups of Agaw, most of whom were major enemies of the Qemant, according to their oral traditions. Finally, the Qemant may have been spared from the Amhara sword simply because they were much less Hebraic than the other Agaw, who were additionally strongly militant in their Hebraism. In short, military social organization and technology did not provide effective boundary-maintaining mechanisms for Agaw groups like the Falasha who, as a result of total defeat by the Amhara, are now dispersed throughout northcentral Ethiopia. Qemant submissiveness coupled with the strict regulation of their behavior by their religion proved more effective for preservation of the group.

Socially and politically the Qemant were only semiautonomous within the Amhara feudal structure, but culturally they were virtually totally independent of Amhara domination and were free to screen out any cultural trait that would disrupt their indigenous sociocultural system. It should be realized that Qemant society could not have exercised its defenses against Amharization without "voluntary" political and economic symbiosis with the Amhara.

Amhara cultural elements that found acceptance were mainly technological. It will be remembered that in the opening centuries of the present millennium, the Agaw had adopted Amhara agricultural technology in preference to their own horticultural and hunting technology. Since stabilized pluralism means arresting the process of assimilation and not curtailing it totally, the Qemant boundary-maintaining mechanisms could not over the centuries screen out a moderate number of nontechnological cultural elements of the Amhara. Thus, through time, a few Christian elements were incorporated in the Qemant religion, and during the first half of the nineteenth century, Amhara personal names were used in preference to Qemant names.

During the long initial phase of Amharization, the only possible avenue of rapid acculturation of the Qemant would have been through the destruction of their religion and its associated defense mechanisms. Given only the sociocultural circumstances found in the Amhara-Qemant milieu of the time, a state of stabilized pluralism allowing only a very slow process of assimilation would likely have endured for many additional centuries. However, new outside factors inducing change were to be added.

Maximal Amharization and the Rupture of the Societal Defense Mechanisms

Initial Amharization of the Qemant continued through the reign of Emperor Theodore II (1855–1868), who had close and loyal Qemant vassals. In fact, Qemant still recount stories about the numerous times they aided him and about the favors this emperor granted to them. Following this period, the religious organization of the Qemant was partially destroyed by force during the reign of Emperor Johannes IV (1872–1889), a militant Christian zealot, and in this way, the Qemant sociocultural system was opened to complete Amharization.

During the reign of Johannes, the independence of Abyssinia was threatened by Egypt, by the Dervishes of the Mahdi in the Sudan, and by various European powers, especially Italy. When some of the encroaching powers appealed to Abyssinian Muslims for support, the emperor decided to unify his religiously diverse subjects. He ordered the Muslims, the pagan-Hebraic Qemant, the Hebrao-pagan Falasha, and the Muslim-pagan Wayto to become baptized as Christians, enforcing his order by use of troops equipped with modern, European firearms.

Enforced Amharization was especially successful against the Qemant, and this program of change initiated the maximal phase of Amharization of these people. The populations of the Muslims, and even the Falasha, were large and dispersed, but the Qemant were relatively few in number and concentrated in a small area. Living around the Amhara center of Gondar, and having rights to land in that area which could be threatened, they were particularly vulnerable to pressure from the Amhara. Some Qemant were converted to Christianity by force of arms or by threats to their rights to land. Johannes encouraged converts to remain Christians by giving them exemptions from taxes on land. To induce religious conversion, he removed from Karkar, the chief religious center of the Qemant, its status and its obligations to pay taxes as a fief in the feudal system of land tenure. The threats against usufruct worked well with the Qemant, but were not effective against the rootless Falasha, the Wayto hunters, and many of the Muslims, none of whom had land rights.

The effort to convert the Qemant was relaxed after the Dervishes destroyed Christian churches in communities of the Qemant area and in Gondar in 1887 and killed Johannes on the battlefield in 1889. A majority of the Qemant reverted to their old religion, but, for the first time, there were appreciable numbers of Christian Qemant. A sizable minority of the Qemant in Karkar remained Christians in order to keep all of Karkar free of its obligations to pay taxes as a fief. Because of conversions to Christianity, there was a breakdown of the old system under which the inhabitants of the eastern Qemant communities paid tribute to the wambar of Karkar; the western Qemant communities, under the wambar of Chelga, had been affected less by enforced Christianization and continued to pay tribute to him until the 1930s.

One might wonder why baptized Qemant were not ostracized by a wambar, thus barring their way to heaven. There are two reasons. First, tales exist that past wambars had predicted those who were baptized would experience dire events. Nervous peasants reported such statements to the Amhara feudal officials, who predicted that an even surer calamity would befall pagan-Hebraic religious practitioners if they continued such maledictory talk. Second, there had been a gradual equation by the Qemant of their God, Mezgana, with the Christian God, the Heavenly Father and His Son. Other members of the Qemant pantheon were sometimes said to be the same as various holy beings of Christianity. Most important, some Qemant believed that the heavenly paradise of the good could be reached through either the Qemant or the Christian religion. It is possible that Qemant equations of some of their beliefs with those of Christianity were postbaptismal rationalizations of an action taken by coercion or design.

Enforced culture change did not entirely destroy the Qemant religious organization, but it decisively weakened this organizational keystone to the maintenance of Qemant societal boundaries. The Christian Qemant had become a sizable group of persons who, although outside the inner circle of the closed society of the pagan-Hebraic Qemant, were nevertheless tied to them by bonds of kinship and association. Pagan-Hebraic Qemant interacted intimately and continuously with their Christian kith and kin, and the interaction provided a bridge to the surrounding Christian world for the pagan-Hebraic Qemant. Conversion to Christianity represented an economic loss to pagan-Hebraic Qemant society and a decrease in the number of adherents to the indigenous Qemant religion. The pagan-Hebraic Qemant had also suffered loss of power and prestige and the outright destruction of religious and lay positions in their religious organization. These various interrelated circumstances made the way clear for the increased Amharization of the Qemant. The cultural independence and semiautonomy of social life which the Qemant had experienced for many centuries while under political domination of the Amhara steadily eroded from the 1880s on.

The Qemant religion was functionally integrated with the other components of their sociocultural system. When a Qemant left the pagan-Hebraic faith, he accordingly began to relinquish many other elements of Qemant culture. Only parts of these elements were transmitted to his children, and usually fewer, if any, to his grandchildren. As Amharization progressed, unilineality and dual social organization with their associated strict laws of marriage were abandoned, as was allegiance to the Qemant politicoreligious leaders. Taboos involving menstruation and childbirth ceased to be observed. Neighboring peoples were no longer considered ritually polluted; thus, it was not necessary to maintain practices of avoiding them. Pagan-Hebraic rites of passage and other religious ceremonies, which imparted a sense of group solidarity, could no longer reach everyone in the community.

Next, we should consider why so many Qemant were Amharized so rapidly. The answer lies in a tendency to accept change which is congruent or compatible with pre-existing cultural traits. Culture change will be accepted if it: (1) is similar to elements already existing in the culture, (2) can be readily integrated into a pattern of culture elements already extant, and (3) does not conflict with existing culture elements or patterns to the degree that the innovation is dysfunctional. Many ancient cultural traits of the Agaw found in Qemant culture were replaced by Amhara counterparts which were congruent, because of common origins, and thus the traits met with acceptance. (See Chapter 2 for information on these common origins and on the cultural fusions resulting in the Amhara culture.) Once the first pressure to change had been forcefully applied and had disrupted the vital societal defense mechanisms, assimilation of the Qemant by the Amhara proceeded rapidly because congruent patterns of culture in the two groups were allowed to coalesce. The relationship between the Agaw and the Amhara is, thus, an example of cultural assimilation brought about by a dominant culture in part through similarities in the two cultures. This congruence may account for the ease with which Qemant equated pagan-Hebraic and Christian holy beings.

The Qemant continued to become acculturated toward the Amhara model, even after Johannes' directed program of cultural change was deemphasized under later rulers. The acculturation process now progressed at a much faster pace than during the initial period of Amharization, when change was held tightly in check by the functional interlocking of boundary-maintaining mechanisms. By the 1930s, a majority of the Qemant still retained their old culture and society, but they were steadily converting to Christianity. Approximately half of the people in the eastern Qemant communities under the wambar of Karkar were probably at least nominal Christians at this time. The Qemant religion was maintained during this period by the support of many Christian Qemant who were recent converts to Christianity and continued to observe various pagan-Hebraic customs. Most of the recent converts elected to contribute to and participate in ceremonies, although they stood apart from the unconverted Qemant during the rites. This practice continues to some extent today in the communities around Chelga.

Qemant may, without severe reprimand from the Amhara, fall back upon the "old religion," especially upon rituals seeking to dispel anxiety or to control the environment. This, again, is made possible through congruence with Amhara culture, which has strong pagan and Hebraic syncretisms in its version of the Christian religion.

The Ethiopian Orthodox Church began a second program of enforced Amharization after the Italian occupation ended in the early 1940s. The ultimate aim, as in the earlier program, was to unify ethnically diverse Ethiopia so that it could resist penetration by a foreign power. Unbaptized Qemant were again threatened with loss of use rights to their land. This program was also directed toward people of other minor ethnic groups of central-western Ethiopia, most of whom have by now undergone Christian baptism, but are at best only partially Amharized. During the program, a zealous proselytizer instigated a mandatory mass baptism of the Qemant which carried their Amharization from the maximal phase into the terminal phase.

Terminal Amharization

The terminal phase of Amharization of the Qemant, which continues today, was well under way by 1950; at this time, only about one thousand Qemant were still unbaptized, and they alone preserved Agaw paganism. These Qemant were usually members of the priestly lineages of the Keber and Yetanti moieties, whose religious zeal persisted despite threats of loss of usufruct and the use of physical force. Finally, appeals by these people to the Ethiopian government led to a decree which allowed them to follow their old religious beliefs and practices without hindrance.

Nevertheless, the Qemant way of life cannot be greatly prolonged by the religious fervor of these few zealots, because the Qemant sociocultural system is no longer truly viable. Demographic conditions, as well as other factors, are now against the perpetuation of the old way of life; the relatively few Qemant still practicing the "old religion" do not fill enough positions in their society to maintain the social interaction necessary for perpetuation of Qemant culture into future generations. A greater number of people are required to support and to participate in the necessary religious events—rites of passage such as the *tazkar*, and rites of intensification such as the spring fertility rite—and to supply sustenance to the members of the priesthood. The most insurmountable problem resulting from inadequate numbers is that pagan-Hebraic Qemant cannot find marriage partners for their children in accordance with the strict and complex marriage laws. One lower priest had to allow his two daughters to become baptized as Christians in order to get husbands for them. Even the wambar's wife is worried about finding husbands of the pagan-Hebraic faith for her daughters. Since Qemant are compelled to marry Christian neighbors in order to avoid what they consider to be incestuous marriages that bring on super-natural sanctions, the end of Qemant society seems imminent.

Today, there are about five-hundred pagan-Hebraic Qemant, but virtually all of these people will have died or have become Christians within the next three decades. Christian Qemant will probably lose most vestiges of their pagan-Hebraic culture within a few decades and will then be on the verge of total assimilation into Amhara society, which totals several million people. Those who have been baptized are still referred to as "Qemant," but this identification, too, will pass with total Amharization. Christian Qemant still constitute part of the Qemant group and possess some group feeling. They maintain a moderate social, if no longer much of a cultural, separateness from the Amhara, but it is very much less than the social distinction between pagan-Hebraic Qemant and the Amhara. This moderate social separation of the Christian Qemant is presently due to practices of marriage and not to customs of excluding outsiders. Qemant marriages continue to follow established lines of kinship, in part for lack of potential marriage partners who are not Qemant. However, group endogamy will not last for long, and the slight social distinction of the Qemant will also doubtless disappear when the Qemant region undergoes the effects of indus-trialization and urbanization in the next few decades.

Amharization as an Acculturative Process

The reader might wonder why almost no mention is made of elements of Westernization in the Amharization of the Qemant. The process of industrialization and urbanization (modernization) begun by the West is reaching most of the societies of the world, and this process will soon be felt throughout Ethiopia. However, in a developing country such as Ethiopia, industrialization does not necessarily mean massive concentration of industry in urban areas. Instead, the industrial wellsprings of modernization in Ethiopia may be geographically remote, situated in other nations, but the influence toward cultural change may be forceful and near at hand as the result of modern forms of communication and transportation. In the Qemant region, for example, future, local modernization will probably see such innovations as new methods of distribution and communication, scientific techniques of agriculture, popular education, and programs of public health, as well as increased bureaucratic centralization and the end of local feudal autonomy. However, the disseminating source of this modernization will for the rest of this century be almost entirely in Europe and North America.

The very nature of industrial urbanization creates a new order of sociocultural change in which every ethnic group will in some way produce for and be dependent upon the world market. It is also an order of change in which the boundaries and identities of many groups, including some of those in Ethiopia, will fade and become lost.

The Qemant, or their totally Amharized descendants, will be no exception to the far-reaching effects of modernization. Until the present, however, they have been essentially unaffected by the global processes of change. Only a few trade goods made by machine are now found among the Qemant: glassware and metal kettles for drinking and serving beer, umbrellas, some items of male clothing, and a few hand tools. The diet of the Qemant remains unchanged and appears to have changed little during the past several centuries. A rare handful of Qemant have abandoned agriculture for government employment and residence in Gondar. A limited number of children in a few communities now attend schools, the largest and best of which are in Gondar. Only a dozen or so Qemant of the last generation were formally educated, and they are no longer rural residents. Attitudes toward mechanical devices may be summed up by recounting the belief that machinery, which is always associated with Europeans, is powered or driven by *Saytan*. Although the Italian operators of satanic machines built in Karkar a water reservoir for Gondar and a now desolate kiln for making bricks, and constructed the main provincial road through the western edge of the Qemant enclave, the Qemant were not employed in these projects and had little contact with Italians or Italian culture.

Traits of culture associated with industrialization will reach the Qemant only as they reach the dominant Amhara. A traditional society is often defined as one existing before contact with the greatly dynamic process of industrial urbanization. Qemant society, therefore, is today a traditional society in which some traditional patterns of culture, such as pagan-Hebraism, are being replaced by other traditional patterns, such as Ethiopian Christianity.

The Amharization of other Ethiopian peoples in relation to Amharization of the Qemant and related Agaw groups is worth noting. The reason why most Agaw groups have been so effectively Amharized, often to the point of total assimilation, is that they have had continuous contact with the Amhara over a span of many centuries, and their acculturation has been further encouraged by congruences between the two cultures. All of the present-day Agaw groups except the Qemant, Falasha, and Kumfal retain little of their Agaw sociocultural heritage that is evident to casual inspection beyond a bilingualism which allows "in group" use of an Agaw dialect. Retention of the Agaw language does provide a rather weak societal boundary that distinguishes these groups from their dominant Amhara or Tegre neighbors, who are not markedly distinct from them in any other way.

Amharization has not and probably will not affect various other ethnic groups of Ethiopia as drastically as it has affected the Agaw. For example, William Shack notes (1966:202) that the Amharization of the Semitic-speaking Gurage peoples does not entail industrial urbanization, and he goes on to state that the "adoption of Amhara customs and values is not necessarily a vehicle of assimilation" for the Gurage (1966:203). Of the non-Agaw peoples, only the northernmost groups of East Cushitic-speaking Galla approach complete Amharization, which seems to have come about voluntarily on the part of the Galla. Allegiance for the past three centuries to the Amhara had political and economic advantages for these Galla, who were intruders in northern and central Ethiopia.

Although Amharization, a process of culture change emanating from a preindustrial civilization, has had relatively little effect to date on non-Agaw peoples, much change will doubtless occur in these societies in the coming decade. Amharization will be gradually modified by industrialization, and the result will eventually be a form of industrial urbanization with an Amhara bent. When this transformation takes place, industrial urban technology and organization will enable a "modernized" Amhara culture to begin assimilation of the great number of cultures within the Ethiopian state, leading to a nation that is culturally more homogeneous.

References and Recommended Reading

The starred works are references cited. All recommended readings are annotated.
A few items in French, German, and Italian have been included because of the relative scarcity of relevant materials in English about the Qemant region. Works containing more than one or two pages on the Qemant are few, but good references to the culture area of Ethiopia and the Horn of Africa are included below. Specific page references to the Qemant in books of the eighteenth and nineteenth centuries will be found in the text of the last section of Chapter 1.

* BARNETT, H. G., 1965, "Laws of Socio-Cultural Change." *International Journal of Comparative Sociology*, 6(2):207–230.
* BEALS, RALPH, 1953, "Acculturation." In *Anthropology Today*, A. L. Kroeber, ed., Chicago: The University of Chicago Press, pp. 621–641.
* BRUCE, JAMES, 1790, *Travels to Discover the Source of the Nile in the Years 1768–73*. Edinburgh: G. G. J. and J. Robinson, 5 vols.
  A lengthy, interesting, and fairly reliable account of life and events in northern and central Ethiopia and the earliest major work on Ethiopia written in English. Several recent one-volume abridgments exist.
BUDGE, E. A., 1928, *A History of Ethiopia*. London: Methuen, 2 vols.
  Recently reprinted and one of the best works on Ethiopian history despite its age. Good references to the Agaw in history and Hebraism in Ethiopia.
BUXTON, DAVID, 1949, *Travels in Ethiopia*. New York: McBride.
  Perhaps the best, and certainly one of the most readable, accounts of travel, local peoples, and religious edifices. New edition appeared in 1967.
CERULLI, ERNESTA, 1956, *Peoples of South-West Ethiopia and its Borderland*. London: International African Institute (Ethnographic Survey of Africa. North-Eastern Africa, Part 3).
  Brief outlines of the ethnic groups of culturally diverse southwestern Ethiopia and Sudan borderlands with a very good bibliography.
CHEESMAN, ROBERT E., 1936, *Lake Tana and the Blue Nile. An Abyssinian Quest*. New York: Macmillan.
  An absorbing and informative account of the first comprehensive exploration of Lake Tana and the Blue Nile, just a few decades ago, by Major Cheesman. Recently reprinted.
CLARK, J. DESMOND, 1954, *The Prehistoric Cultures of the Horn of Africa*. New York: Cambridge.
  The standard work on the industries of the stone ages in Ethiopia and Somaliland by the dean of African archaeology. Most certainly the first book one should read on the area.
* CONSOCIAZIONE TURISTICA ITALIANA, 1938, *Guida dell'Africa Orientale Italiana*. Milan: Consociazione Turistica Italiana.
  Although not up to date, this is still the best guide, tourist or otherwise, to Ethiopia. Considerable information on geography and places of historic interest and good regional and town maps.
CONTI ROSSINI, CARLO, 1912, "La Langue des Kemant en Abyssinie." *Kaiserliche Akademie der Wissenschaften, Schriften der Sprachenkommission*, 4:1–316.

A good Qemantinya-French dictionary with an adequate grammar. The first thirty pages are a summary of the literature published on the Qemant until 1912.

DORESSE, JEAN, 1959, *Ethiopia*. London: Elek Books.

A thorough, recently written history of Ethiopia, focused on the Semitic-speaking peoples.

* FLAD, JOHANN M. A., 1866, *A Short Description of the Falashas and Kamants in Abyssinia*. Chrishona: The Mission Press.

* ———, 1869, *The Falashas (Jews) of Abyssinia*, S. P. Goodhart, trans. London: Wm. Macintosh.

Two works with a little information on the Qemant and a greater amount on the related Falasha, including vocabularies of their common language.

GAMST, FREDERICK C., 1965, "Travel and Research in Northwestern Ethiopia." *Notes for Anthropologists and other Field Workers in Ethiopia*, No. 2. Addis Ababa: Institute of Ethiopian Studies, Haile Sellassie I University.

Account of procedures for arriving in Ethiopia and for obtaining permission and documents and outfitting for fieldwork. Ethnographic and archaeological potentials of the area are outlined and a bibliography useful in preparation for fieldwork in Ethiopia is included. Condition and/or availability of roads, trails, lodging, food, supplies, and gasoline are noted enroute to and within Bagemder and Semen.

* GOBAT, SAMUEL, 1834, *Journal of a Three Years' Residence in Abyssinia*. London: Hatchard & Son; and Seeley & Sons.

GREENBERG, JOSEPH H., 1963, "The Languages of Africa." *International Journal of American Linguistics*, 29(1:2):1–171.

A basic work in African linguistics summarizing the Afro-Asiatic languages, including Ethiopian Semitic and Cushitic tongues.

HALÉVY, J., 1877, "Travels in Abyssinia." J. Picciotto, trans. In *Miscellany of Hebrew Literature*, 2(Series 2), A. L. Löwy, ed. London: Trübner and Co., pp. 175–256.

An account of the Falasha by one of the first scholars to stimulate European interest in these people and to comment on the proselytizing of Flad and other missionaries among the Falasha and Qemant.

* HEUGLIN, MARTIN T. VON, 1868, *Reise nach Abessinien*. Jena: Hermann Costenoble.

HUNTINGFORD, G. W. B., 1955, *The Galla of Ethiopia*. London: International African Institute (Ethnographic Survey of Africa. North-Eastern Africa, Part 2).

Outline of the numerous Galla-speaking groups who have an estimated population of 8 million and accounts of the walled kingdoms of Kafa and Janjero in southern Ethiopia, with very good bibliographies.

———, 1965, *The Glorious Victories of Amda Seyon King of Ethiopia*. New York: Oxford.

A modern translation into English of one of the many Imperial Chronicles of Abyssinia; manuscripts written in Geez. Most such translations are into Latin, French, and German.

JÄGER, OTTO A., 1965, *Antiquities of North Ethiopia*. Stuttgart: F. A. Brockhaus.

An informative guide to the historic ruins and historic structures still in use of Semitic-speaking Ethiopia.

LEIRIS, MICHEL, 1958, *La Possession et ses Aspects Theatraux chez les Ethiopiens de Gondar*. Paris: Librairie Plon.

The most exhaustive study on shamanism and *zar* possession in the Qemant area.

LEROY, JULES, S. WRIGHT, and O. A. JÄGER, 1961, *Ethiopia: Illuminated Manuscripts*. Greenwich, Conn.: New York Graphic Society (UNESCO World Art Series).

A fascinating and superbly illustrated book on the art work of the manuscripts of medieval Abyssinia.

LESLAU, WOLF, 1951, *Falasha Anthology*. New Haven: Yale University Press.

A short ethnography of the Falasha based on the author's fieldwork is followed by translation from the Geez of religious books unique to these people. Includes the *Teezaza Sanbat*, an account of a personified female Sabbath.

LEVINE, DONALD N., 1965, *Wax and Gold. Tradition and Innovation in Ethiopian Culture*. Chicago: University of Chicago Press.
A study breaking new social scientific ground in analyses of Amhara culture and psychology.

LEWIS, HERBERT S., 1965, *A Galla Monarchy: Jimma Abba Jifar, Ethiopia, 1830–1932*. Madison: University of Wisconsin Press.
A fresh contribution to political anthropology with a structural study of a southern Ethiopian Kingdom. Based on the author's fieldwork and extensive knowledge of Ethiopia and the Horn.

LEWIS, I. M., 1955, *Peoples of the Horn of Africa. Somali, Afar and Saho*. London: International African Institute (Ethnographic Survey of Africa. North-Eastern Africa, Part 1).
Outline, with very good bibliographies, of cultures of the various Somali groups and of the Afar and Saho peoples to the north of them.

———, 1961, *A Pastoral Democracy; a Study of Pastoralism and Politics among the Northern Somali of the Horn of Africa*. New York, Oxford.
The best single study of the Somali who are several million in number. Based upon many years of fieldwork by the author.

* MURDOCK, GEORGE P., 1949, *Social Structure*. New York: Macmillan.

———, 1959, *Africa. Its Peoples and Their Culture History*. New York: McGraw-Hill.
Chapters 22 through 26 of this thought-provoking encyclopedic work provide an excellent background to the past cultural achievement of the Cushitic-speaking peoples of eastern Africa. Pages 181–84 note the importance of the Agaw, considered by Murdock "as one of the culturally most creative peoples on the entire continent."

* MESSING, SIMON D., 1958, "Group Therapy and Social Status in the Zar Cult of Ethiopia." *American Anthropologist*, 60:1120–1126.
A thorough analysis of some aspects of *zar*. Based upon the author's fieldwork in and around Gondar.

PANKHURST, RICHARD, 1961, *An Introduction to the Economic History of Ethiopia from Early Time to 1800*. London: Lalibela House.
A very readable history of Ethiopia focused on economics and political organization; a study, with an important bibliography, making a most scholarly use of the literature on Ethiopia.

PERHAM, MARGERY, 1948, *The Government of Ethiopia*. London: Faber.
Despite the passage of the years, still the best work on the political structure of Ethiopia.

* RASSAM, HORMUZD, 1869, *Narrative of the British Mission to Theodore, King of Abyssinia*. London: J. Murray, 2 vols.

RATHJENS, CARL, 1921, *Die Juden in Abessinien*. Hamburg: W. Gente, Wissenschaftlicher Verlag.
An early and perceptive work on Hebraism in Ethiopia and Ethiopian religions. Author's experience limited to northern Ethiopia; he did not visit Qemant or Falasha areas.

* RÜPPEL, EDUARD, 1838–1840, *Reise in Abessinien*. Frankfurt a/M: S. Schmerber, 2 vols.

SAHLE SELLASSIE, 1964, *Shinega's Village. Scenes of Ethiopian Life*. Wolf Leslau, trans. Berkeley: University of California Press.
A novel, translated from Chaha, containing perceptive insights into Gurage village life and problems of modernization among these people.

* SHACK, WILLIAM A., 1966, *The Gurage: Peoples of the Ensete Culture*. London: Oxford (published for the International African Institute).
A stimulating book based upon extensive fieldwork; the first comprehensive social anthropological study in English of an Ethiopian people.

* SIMOONS, FREDERICK J., 1960, *Northwest Ethiopia; Peoples and Economy.* Madison: University of Wisconsin Press.

An ethnography and cultural geography of the province containing Qemantland; a highly interesting, well-illustrated, and well-rounded study based on the author's fieldwork.

* STERN, HENRY A., 1862, *Wanderings among the Falashas in Abyssinia.* London: Wertheim, Macintosh, and Hunt.

Recently reprinted, but not too rewarding to the reader interested in the Qemant, Falasha, or Ethiopia.

TRIMINGHAM, J. SPENCER, 1965, *Islam in Ethiopia.* London: Frank Cass & Co. (First published in 1952).

Despite the title, this book is a comprehensive history of Ethiopia containing information on pagan-Agaw and Hebraic religion as well. Excellent use of the literature on Ethiopia.

TUBIANA, JOSEPH, 1959, "Note sur la Distribution Geographique des Dialectes Agaw." In *Mer Rouge—Afrique Orientale. Cahiers de l'Afrique et de l'Asie,* 5:297–306.

Survey of Agaw groups and their dialects by a scholar who has done linguistic fieldwork among the Qemant.

TUCKER, ARCHIBALD N., and M. A. BRYAN, 1966, *Linguistic Analysis; the non-Bantu Languages of North-Eastern Africa.* London: Oxford (published for the International African Institute).

Along with Greenberg's study, one of the basic books on African languages; contains important analysis of Cushitic and Semitic languages in Ethiopia.

ULLENDORFF, EDWARD, 1956, "Hebraic-Jewish Elements in Abyssinian (Monophysite) Christianity." *Journal of Semitic Studies,* 1:216–256.

The best summary and analysis of Hebraism in Ethiopian Christianity.

———, 1960, *The Ethiopians.* New York: Oxford.

An outstanding short introduction to Ethiopia with a chapter on the history of Ethiopian studies.